D1475350

MORMON
NEO-ORTHODOXY:

A CRISIS THEOLOGY.

———————

MORMON NEO-ORTHODOXY:

A CRISIS THEOLOGY.

BY

O. KENDALL WHITE, JR.

SALT LAKE CITY, UTAH.

1987.

COPYRIGHT 1987 SIGNATURE BOOKS, INC.

SIGNATURE BOOKS IS A RECOGNIZED TRADEMARK OF

SIGNATURE BOOKS, INC.

PRINTED IN THE UNITED STATES OF AMERICA

ALL RIGHTS RESERVED

SECOND PRINTING 1988

BOOK DESIGN BY MAXINE HANKS

COVER DESIGN BY LEGUME + ASSOCIATES

COVER PHOTO: THE MORMON TABERNACLE CHOIR

IN THE KIRTLAND TEMPLE, 1911

WHITE, O. KENDALL. MORMON NEO-ORTHODOXY.

BIBLIOGRAPHY: P. INCLUDES INDEX.

1. CHURCH OF JESUS CHRIST OF LATTER-DAY SAINTS - DOCTRINES.

2. MORMON CHURCH - DOCTRINES. 3. NEO-ORTHODOXY. I. TITLE.

BX8635.2.W53. 1987. 306'.6. 87-12706.

ISBN: 0-941214-52-4.

TO MY PARENTS
Thelma Clark White and Owen Kendall White
who epitomize the best of
traditional Mormonism.

TABLE OF CONTENTS.

PREFACE . . . . ix.

INTRODUCTION . . . . xi.

I. THE DEVELOPMENT OF CRISIS THEOLOGIES . 1.

II. PROTESTANT NEO-ORTHODOXY . . . . 27.

III. TRADITIONAL MORMON THEOLOGY . . . 57.

IV. MORMON NEO-ORTHODOXY . . . . . 89.

V. RECENT DEVELOPMENTS . . . . . . 139.

CONCLUSION . . . . 159.

BIBLIOGRAPHY . . . . 177.

PREFACE.

M y interest in Mormon neo-orthodox theology began in the mid-1960s with my own religious questions regarding Mormonism. I became attracted to both the philosophy and sociology of religion and enjoyed the unique opportunity of studying with such scholars of religion in general and Mormonism in particular as Thomas F. O'Dea, Sterling M. McMurrin, Waldemer P. Read, Lewis Max Rogers, Lowell L. Bennion, and Ray R. Canning. I am profoundly indebted to each of these men for enabling me to address my interests within the context of my own religious tradition. During my undergraduate and graduate years, I was struck by parallels between certain Mormon writers and the theologies of Protestants whom I was studying and was able to convince my thesis committee, despite some skepticism from a few members, of the value of a sociological study of Mormon neo-orthodoxy as an emerging theology.

My current religious position as well as my research on Mormonism have been shaped by numerous conversations with my brothers—Bill Humphrey and Brent and Daryl White—and with my cousin, the late Glenn White. (Daryl also deserves my thanks for a cover design we were unable to use.) To them and my parents, who I am confident have heard more discussions of Mormon theologies than they probably wish, I express my appreciation. Wayland Hand, an uncle and scholar *par excellence*, provided valuable criticism and encouragement for all of my Mormon research. He wanted to purchase the first copy of this book, and I deeply regret that he did not live to see it published. I have also enjoyed a wonderful life with a dear friend, a perceptive analyst of our respective Mormon backgrounds, and a wonderful critic of my research and writing. To my wife, Arlene Burraston-White, who can only imagine the depth of my appreciation, I am especially grateful.

Finally, I wish to thank Kent Robson, Daniel Rector, and Richard Sherlock for their comments and criticisms, as well as Gary J. Bergera, Ronald Priddis, Susan Staker, and the staff at Signature Books. Their knowledge of the subject matter, assistance with the manuscript, and encouragement of the project exceeded my greatest expectations. At the same time, I would not want to convey the idea that all of us necessarily see eye-to-eye on Protestant, Mormon, and neo-Mormon theology, and I alone am responsible for the discussion and conclusions that follow.

1987.   K.W.

INTRODUCTION.

The sociology of religion examines religious beliefs within their social contexts. Certain social conditions are conducive to specific religious beliefs: while the affluence of upper classes encourages religions which legitimize the existing social order, the poverty of lower classes inspires ethical and salvation religions. Social or cultural crises often function as midwives for the birth of theologies which project human hopes onto another world, promise future rewards for present suffering, vigorously defend existing dogmas, and deny any possibility that humans may overcome their predicament. For the purpose of my analysis, these will be classified as "crisis literature."

This book describes a contemporary theological development in Mormonism—which I have called Mormon neo-orthodoxy—and examines the cultural milieu out of which it emerged. Affirming the fundamental doctrines of the sovereignty of God, the depravity of human nature, and salvation by grace, Mormon neo-orthodoxy may be closer to Protestant fundamentalism and neo-orthodoxy than to what I and others esteem to be traditional Mormon thought. Like these Protestant movements, Mormon neo-orthodoxy is a response to the experience of "modernity"—the secularization of society and culture. Thus

Protestant neo-orthodoxy and Mormon neo-orthodoxy are crisis theologies.

The theologies of Swiss theologian Karl Barth and German philosopher H. Emil Brunner—the principal architects of Protestant neo-orthodoxy—are similar to the Reformation theologies of Martin Luther and John Calvin. However, Protestant neo-orthodoxy did not merely restate Reformation theology. Rather it reinterpreted Reformation doctrines in the context of modern life and thereby attempted to recapture the spirit and "truth" elucidated by Luther and Calvin. No other theologians, except possibly Augustine, had so clearly described the "true nature of the human predicament." If Luther and Calvin were too literalistic in their treatment of scripture, they nonetheless recognized the profound "otherness" of God, the absolute helplessness of human beings, and the necessity of grace if humanity were to be saved from its fallen state. From this emphasis on the doctrines of classical Protestantism, Protestant neo-orthodoxy derived its name.

Until the early years of the twentieth century, Protestant liberalism, a product of the Enlightenment, was perhaps Christianity's most promising theological development with its celebration of science and reason. Some liberal Protestants came to see God as an ideal—the embodiment of the finest human values—while others regarded him as a finite being. Virtually all liberal Protestants espoused an optimistic conception of human nature. Through moral and rational progress humanity would solve many of its prob-

lems. The Kingdom of God as a just, peaceful, and harmo-
nious society had become a real possibility, requiring only
the adequate development of reason, science, and technology. Instead of awaiting the direct intervention of Christ
the Redeemer, liberalism depended on the example of Jesus
the teacher. The good society would result from humans
acting out the moral teachings of Christianity.

This avowedly optimistic world view was a casualty
of World War I. That leaders of modern, civilized nations—
supposedly far removed from "primitive savages"—could
not resolve their differences peaceably convinced Barth and
Brunner of the inherent evil in human nature. World War I
provided them with empirical evidence of the failure of reason and moral accommodation. But if the "war to end all
wars" had vanquished optimism in Europe, it was not sufficient to destroy American optimism which survived until
the advent of the Great Depression. The 1932 publication
of Reinhold Niebuhr's *Moral Man and Immoral Society*
brought Protestant neo-orthodox theology to American
shores. In a devastating critique of Protestant liberalism and
secular rationalism, Neibuhr defended fundamental premises
of Reformation Christianity, especially the doctrine of original sin in his pessimistic concept of human nature.

Given this reaction to the experience of modernity
and the concern of Barth and Brunner with the "crisis of
God's judgment upon the world," this new theology was
also called Protestant crisis theology. Other names included
kerygmatic theology, dialectical theology, theology of the

Word, the new-supernaturalism, and neo-fundamentalism. However, Protestant neo-orthodoxy remained the most popular name because it restated Refomation theology in a modern context, while departing from Protestant fundamentalism by accepting modern biblical scholarship and non-literal approaches to scripture.

Emerging from the optimism of the nineteenth century, Mormonism, or the Church of Jesus Christ of Latter-day Saints, as it is officially known today, was likewise forced to negotiate the traumas of modernity, effecting a unique synthesis of American religious and secular culture. In nineteenth-century Mormonism, Christian beliefs combined with contemporary science. Though generally assuming a posture of scriptural literalism, Mormon theology was surprisingly liberal. An optimistic concept of human potential and the notion of progress so characteristic of Protestant liberalism and American culture became the foundation of the profound "this worldliness" of Mormon theology. Proclaiming that Jesus would only return to a community built upon principles of equality, order, and justice, Mormons fused the religious enthusiasm embodied in Christian eschatology with the immediacy of secular reform. Millennial expectations became the basis of a this-worldly theology, and the energy projected by other-worldly religions onto an after-life became the basis for the collective transformation of this world. Mundane activities were infused with religious significance, and building the good society became a social obligation. A religion that could not save humanity in this world could hardly be expected to do so in the next. Thus, in theology and practice, Mormonism came to repudiate the discontinuity inherent in the Protestant preoccupation with divine "otherness" and human depravity.

In 1922 Mormon philosopher E. E. Ericksen reflected on the status of these beliefs in the twentieth century. In the first social-scientific study of Mormonism, Ericksen argued that repeated conflicts with non-Mormons and with nature had shaped the development of nineteenth-century Mormonism's social ethics and theology. Similarly, twentieth-century Mormon theology reflected further accommodation to the larger, surrounding society. Some of the most fundamental concepts of nineteenth-century Mormonism were reinterpreted to meet new social realities. Thus a concept like the Kingdom of God, which originally referred to the ideal society that the newly "gathered" Saints would build, became the church or an other-worldly institution to be established in an indeterminate future. That which was originally concrete and real had been mystified and relegated to the realm of metaphysics.

However, these theological innovations, though demonstrating Mormonism's capacity for adaptation, failed to reveal the depth of the problem. For Ericksen, accommodation had also produced a conflict between "new ideas and old institutions." Apologists defending the new dogmas had already emerged, and church officials had begun to differentiate Mormonism from modern, secular society.

This cultural challenge to the beliefs that give meaning and purpose to social order would persist through the next several decades. In the post-World War II era, it would become the principal preoccupation of Mormon leaders and would encourage the formulation of Mormon neo-orthodox theology.

Mormons have traditionally believed in a finite God, an optimistic assessment of human nature, and a doctrine of salvation by merit. In contrast, most Mormon neo-orthodox theologians have tended to embrace the concept of an absolute God, a pessimistic assessment of human nature, and a doctrine of salvation by grace. As early as 1962, LDS educator George T. Boyd called the attention of his colleagues to a new "Mormon" concept of human nature. There would be little reason for writing about "the moral nature of man," he declared, were it "not for the fact that within recent years there has been a negation of man . . . in both religious and secular circles" (1962, 1). Both a "revived Protestant Fundamentalism" and an "agnostic naturalism" imply that the "moral nature of man is somewhat of an illusion." While each school of thought has had some influence on the church, Boyd argued that

> only the former, which paradoxically enough seeks to honor God by debasing man whom he created in his image, finds any influential expression or hearing within the Church.
>
> This neo-Calvinism which with increasing frequency zealously proclaims the depravity of man has much in common with the doctrine of Saint Augustine who was

one of the chief creators of the original heresy. And, as the doctrine of Augustine tells us more about Augustine than it does the original teachings of Christ relative to God and man so this recently revived negative doctrine of human nature may tell us more about its formulators and defenders than it does about the Mormon doctrine of man and, perhaps, should be ignored. Nevertheless, while such negativism may be a corrective to a superficial liberalism it does represent a threat to Mormon orthodoxy and an obtrusion on established Mormon thought (1962, 2).

In his 1965 lectures on Mormon theology, subsequently published as *The Theological Foundations of the Mormon Religion*, Sterling M. McMurrin, a philosopher at the University of Utah, characterized Mormon theology as a Pelagian heresy because of its emphasis on free will, its optimistic evaluation of human nature, and its doctrine of salvation by works. He detected, however, a "kind of Jansenist movement in Mormon academic circles," with its preoccupation with human depravity and divine grace, that seems "dedicated to the celebration of whatever Augustinian elements may be discernible in the scriptures" (1965, 66-67). In a subsequent lecture, McMurrin argued that this contemporary effort to recast human nature in pessimistic terms suggested parallels with Protestant neo-orthodoxy:

> Although Mormonism has known little of the social and personal failure that has contributed to the success of neoorthodoxy, for the past two decades it has, in common with American and European religion generally, become increasingly conservative in theology. The most interesting facet of this conservatism is a noticeable ten-

dency, especially in Mormon academic circles, to deny the traditional liberalism of Mormon theology by favoring a negative description of human nature and the human predicament. This tendency is more than a criticism of the excessive optimism that has been characteristic of liberalism. It appears to be grounded especially in a strong appetite for traditional orthodoxy that is whetted by a reading of *The Epistle to the Romans* and a taste for those occasional passages like the Mosiah ''enemy of God'' statement which appear in the Mormon scriptures. And it is aided and abetted by the predilection of the orthodox for whatever demeans humanity for the glory of God. But that Mormonism reflects Christian orthodoxy in its treatment of the Bible, and its acceptance of many of the dogmas central to traditional Christianity, does not invalidate its essentially liberal character which is defined by its concepts of man and God. A departure from this fundamental liberalism is a departure from the authentic spirit of the Mormon religion (1965, 111).

Though occasional discussions of this emerging theological phenomenon have appeared in the writings of some Mormon scholars, no systematic analysis of it occurred before 1967 (see White 1967, 1970, 1971a, 1971b, for discussions of Mormon neo-orthodoxy that fail to address its social and cultural context). This book, which attempts to describe both Mormon neo-orthodox theology and the cultural crisis underlying it, also incorporates insights from recent Mormon scholarship dealing with the post-World War II period through the 1980s—the time of origin and formulation of Mormon neo-orthodox theology.

That this theology is primarily a post-World War II phenomenon has been reinforced by historian Thomas G.

Alexander in his seminal analysis of "The Reconstruction of Mormon Doctrine" published in 1980. However, Alexander convincingly argued that during the initial period of the formulation of Mormon doctrine, 1830 to 1835, Mormon beliefs differed little from those of American Protestants. Tempered by the perfectionism of the Methodists, the Mormon doctrine of human nature tended toward depravity, while its absolutist and trinitarian concept of God reinforced a notion of saving grace provided by the death and atonement of Jesus Christ (see also Lyon 1975). As prevalent themes in the Book of Mormon, these were apparently beliefs of the earliest Mormons.

From 1835 until his martrydom in 1844, Joseph Smith increasingly emphasized the finite nature of God, a more optimistic view of humanity, and a doctrine of salvation by merit (Alexander 1980; Lyon 1975). This was Smith's theological legacy that at the hands of the most prominent Mormon theologians—B. H. Roberts, John A. Widtsoe, and James E. Talmage—became the synthesis of traditional Mormonism during the late nineteenth and early twentieth centuries. Even popular mid-twentieth-century conservative theologians like Joseph Fielding Smith, who seems not to have appreciated fully the implications of Joseph Smith's radical departure from Christian orthodoxy, embraced the metaphysics, the optimistic concept of human nature, and the doctrine of salvation (exaltation) by merit of traditional Mormonism. Joseph Fielding Smith's conflicts with Talmage and other traditional Mormons were largely a result of his excessive scriptural literalism.

That the traditional synthesis generally came to be equated with Mormonism is acknowledged even by Mormon neo-orthodox theologians. Both the early and recent generations of neo-orthodox theologians have found themselves battling popularly held views celebrating the goodness of human nature, equating grace with physical resurrection, and demanding that human beings "work out their own salvation" (see Andrus 1961; Yarn 1965; Toscano 1983, 91; Olsen 1984; Voros 1985). Contrasting "redemptive Mormonism" with the "humanistic view," the former being comparable to neo-orthodoxy and the latter to traditional Mormonism, J. Frederic Voros, Jr., a recent neo-orthodox theologian, claims that the "popular hegemony of the humanistic view is nearly complete" and that today "most public church teaching is merely an attempt to inculcate moral precepts." The writings of the Apostle Paul, according to Voros, are generally "dead letters to these Church members" (1985, 1-2).

My use of the term "Mormon neo-orthodoxy" is admittedly arbitrary and may not satisfy everyone. Though my initial usage did not imply a return to early Mormon thought, the analyses of Alexander and T. Edgar Lyon have convinced me that Mormon neo-orthodoxy is similar to Mormon theology of 1830 to 1835. In this sense, it may be conceived as a return to the earliest "Mormon" beliefs and, consequently, as an authentic expression of Mormon theology. However, and this is a fundamental point, it does not represent a return to the theology that Joseph Smith left as his legacy—the theology that became the foundation of traditional Mormonism (see chap. 3).[1]

Some readers may also find my characterization of "traditional Mormonism" too broad. Certainly the historical development of Mormon doctrine does not lend itself easily to generalization. Different teachings have been variously interpreted at different periods of time, although most originate in some form or another in the theology of Joseph Smith. Some "official" doctrines—such as the so-called Adam-God doctrine, plural marriage, and the priesthood ban on blacks—have been discarded, if not repudiated, since

---

[1]Although I use the term "neo-orthodoxy" to suggest an affinity with the tenets of the Protestant movement, this relationship should not be overstated. Mormon neo-orthodoxy differs from Protestant neo-orthodoxy in at least two significant ways: Mormon neo-orthodox theologians tend not to take modern biblical scholarship seriously, while Protestant neo-orthodox theologians do; Mormon theologians generally are scriptural literalists, while Protestants are not. Such differences may imply that "Mormon neo-fundamentalism" would have been a preferable term. However, fundamentalism has a special connotation to most Mormons; it refers to dissenting groups from the church that continue to practice polygamy. While "Mormon crisis theology" offered some appeal, I rejected it because Mormonism has been plagued by crises throughout its history, as reflected in its early teachings and in the later adaptations. In the end, "Mormon neo-orthodoxy" seemed to present the fewest difficulties. I should note that only rarely will any two Mormon theologians, whom I classify as neo-orthodox, agree on all aspects of their theology. What they do seem to share is a belief in the depravity of humanity, salvation by grace, and the sovereignty of God.

they were first announced more than a century ago. Others, such as the identification of God the Father as Elohim and Jesus Christ as Jehovah, only emerged after the death of Joseph Smith. Still, certain core doctrines, including the finite nature of God, the goodness of humanity, and salvation by merit, have persisted in the Mormon church at least since the 1840s. The synthesis of these three basic doctrines into a coherent theology is what I refer to as "traditional Mormonism."

To arrive at my observations and conclusions, I have examined books, articles, papers, and speeches of the Protestant and Mormon neo-orthodox theologians, including some officials of the Mormon church. Occasionally I obtained information from personal conversations with theologians following public addresses or during meetings with small discussion groups. I have made no attempt to assess the distribution of neo-orthodox ideas among Mormons generally or within the academic community. Hence, I make no claims about the proportion of Mormons committed to either traditional Mormon or Mormon neo-orthodox beliefs.

What I do examine is the social and cultural origins of Mormon neo-orthodox theology. I am particularly interested in the impact of "modernity"—the challenge to religion posed by secularization. However, this book should not be read as an analysis of the truth claims of the theologies it discusses. Nor does it adopt either a primarily theological or historical approach to the subject at hand. Rather, it is an exercise in the sociology of religion designed to identify environmental factors influencing the development of the theology. It also briefly discusses some implications neo-orthodoxy may pose for the future of Mormon theology and religion. Some readers may find a certain amount of overlap from one chapter to the next, but given the complexity of some of the issues under discussion, I believe that some repetition is necessary.

In order to understand the conceptual framework for my analysis, chapter 1 presents a general discussion of the relationships among social and cultural phenomena and the emergence of religious beliefs. While it introduces read-ers to some of the classic issues in the sociology of religion, it also develops a theory of crisis theologies. The distinc-tion between social and cultural crises—the former consti-tuting a threat to the physical survival of the group, the latter a challenge to the belief system that infuses social order with meaning—enables us to identify four distinct theological types: apocalypticism, martyrology, apologetics, and neo-orthodoxy. The remainder of the book is devoted to describing and analyzing the latter.

Chapter 2, on Protestant neo-orthodox theology, presents the basic theological tenets of this reformulation of Reformation theology—its preoccupation with the oth-erness of God, the depravity of human nature, and the necessity of salvation by grace—and describes the cultural crisis underlying it. Arguing that an understanding of this cultural crisis is essential to an understanding of the devel-opment of Protestant neo-orthodoxy, this chapter also serves

as a model for the analysis of Mormon neo-orthodox theology in chapter 4.

Chapter 3 describes what I have broadly defined as
traditional Mormon theology. Incorporating the general optimism of American culture and Protestant liberalism, the
Mormon synthesis formulated during the 1840s, and elab-
orated during the latter part of the nineteenth and early
part of the twentieth centuries, proclaimed a metaphysics
that requires a finite God, the fundamental goodness of
human nature, and a doctrine of salvation based primarily
on merit. The radical perfectionism embodied in Mormon
doctrine (that is, the possibility of mortals becoming gods)
provided a foundation for the intellectual and social activ-
ism—the profound this-worldliness—so characteristic of the
Mormon religion.

It is from this liberal optimism that Mormon neo-
orthodox theologians typically dissent. Their theology,
which contains significant parallels to Protestant
neo-orthodoxy, is described in chapter 4, which also presents
an analysis of the cultural crisis confronting modern Mormonism. The anti-intellectual and authoritarian reactions
of some Mormons to secularization are incorporated into a
theology that doubts human capabilities and requires inordinate dependence on external authority. From premises
of human contingency and total helplessness, the doctrines
of divine sovereignty and salvation by grace follow logically. Like their Protestant counterparts, Mormon neo-

orthodox theologians proclaim a "good news" that sounds much like the basic tenets of Reformation theology.

Chapter 5 examines a new generation of Mormon neo-orthodox writers. During the past eight years, several theologians have advanced concepts of God, human nature, and salvation that depend on original sin, human depravity, and the necessity of grace. Explicitly challenging the traditional Mormon preoccupation with works, their doctrine of salvation, which emphasizes "justification" and "sanctification," contains a language that is foreign to Mormon religious discourse and which is even closer to the Protestant tradition than that of their theological predecessors.

A conclusion summarizes my argument, discusses some implications of Mormon neo-orthodoxy for Mormon theology and religion, distinguishes between the social ethics of Protestant and Mormon neo-orthodox theologians, and suggests a primary reason why neo-orthodox ideas may gain greater currency among contemporary Latter-day Saints.

THE DEVELOPMENT OF CRISIS THEOLOGIES.

CHAPTER 1.

When Karl Marx addressed the relationship between social structure and ideas in the mid-nineteenth century, he virtually created the field known today as the sociology of knowledge (see Marx 1909; 1963; 1964). According to Marx, individuals who share the same relationship to the means of production within a society also share interests that influence their ideas and beliefs. Organized into systematic forms, these beliefs are "ideologies" when they perpetuate class interests. By legitimizing the established social order, ideologies help to preserve society.

It is in this context that Marx analyzed religion. His famous proposition—"religion is an opiate of the masses"— referred to the tendency of "other-worldly" religions to deflect the attention of the poor away from the sources of their economic and social problems. By promising a reward in heaven for suffering on earth and stressing that it is more difficult for "a rich man to enter the kingdom of heaven" than "for a camel to pass through the eye of a needle," Christianity contributes, however unintentionally, to the preservation of economic inequality. While such religious beliefs help the poor adjust to their suffering, they inhibit any inclination to change society. These beliefs are ideological because of their tacit acceptance of the position of the ruling class and negation of the economic and social interests of the poor. For Marx, the struggle against religious ideologies was a struggle against the oppression of the poor. Religion was largely a conservative force which functioned to perpetuate the existing social order. In its crudest form, Marxist theory held that ideas were simply products of social relations and conditions.

In response, Max Weber (1958), a brilliant early twentieth-century German sociologist, argued that Calvinistic Protestantism had helped to create modern, Western capitalism. Calvinists, believing in predestination, worked diligently, without spending money or engaging in "sensual cultural" activities, to prove to themselves that they were among the elect. This "Protestant Ethic" of hard work and frugality was, according to Weber, a major factor in the production of modern, western capitalism. So, Weber argued, religious beliefs or ideas had helped to create a new social order. What Marx regarded as effect, Weber identified as cause.

Though additional discussion of Weber's analysis of the Protestant ethic is beyond the scope of this chapter, it is important to note that the debate between Marx and Weber did not mean that Weber was unsympathetic to Marx's general premise. Weber too found social conditions, including class relations, to be significant determinants of beliefs and behavior. Weber shared the assumption of his student, Karl Mannheim, that changing belief systems constitute "a particularly sensitive index of social and cultural change" (Mannheim 1936, 83, 243).

Researchers distinguishing themselves in the sociology of religion have typically been scholars who have contributed to our understanding of relationships among social phenomena and religious belief systems. In one of the finest works in the sociology of religion, H. Richard Niebuhr, a Protestant historian and theologian, challenged the traditional notion that denominationalism had its origins in theological disputes by pointing instead to the social, political, and economic differences dividing various groups. According to Niebuhr, these divergent theologies were rationalizations of deeper social cleavages and not the fundamental causes of schisms within the Protestant community:

> Less directly, but none the less effectively, theological opinions have their roots in the relationship of the religious life to the cultural and political conditions prevailing in any group of Christians. This does not mean that an economic or purely political interpretation of theology is justified, but it does mean that the religious life is so interwoven with social circumstances that the formation of theology is necessarily conditioned by these (1929, 15–16).

Even a cursory examination of the literature in the sociology of religion, including the writings of Weber, Marx, and Niebuhr, establishes a connection between an individual's position within society and the religious beliefs he holds. Both Weber and Niebuhr speak of religions of the "privileged" and "nonprivileged" classes. As one's social and psychological needs differ, so too do his or her religious beliefs. Referring to the religion of the privileged classes, Weber notes:

> Other things being equal, classes with high social and economic privilege will scarcely be prone to evolve the idea of salvation. Rather, they assign to religion the primary function of legitimizing their own life pattern and situation in the world. This universal phenomenon is rooted in certain basic psychological patterns. When a man who is happy compares his position with that of one who is unhappy, he is not content with the fact of his happiness, but desires something more, namely the right to this happiness, the consciousness that he has earned his good fortune, in contrast to the unfortunate who must equally have earned his misfortune (1963, 107).

On the other hand, nonprivileged classes, as victims of oppression, tend to project their needs for assistance onto a salvation religion having other-worldly implications. Indeed, Weber demonstrated that the lower the class the more radical the "forms assumed by the need for a savior, once this need has emerged" (1963, 102). Since the allocation of material goods delineates social class, it is the most significant of the various factors enhancing the social distance between the lower and upper classes (Niebuhr 1929, 26). According to Niebuhr, this economic factor, operating directly and indirectly, has been the major influence in creating the schisms within Christian churches.

If these are the functions of religions of the upper and lower classes, what about religions of the middle class? Do they legitimize a social position or promise salvation? The answer depends upon the relationship of the middle class to the other classes. When the middle class is in a fairly stable position, it is unlikely to advocate an ethical or salvation religion (Weber 1963, 90–92). However, when struggling for social recognition or legitimacy and resenting both upper and lower classes, the middle class may embrace an ethical or salvation religion. Thus Erich Fromm characterized John Calvin's preoccupation with a God "who wants unrestricted power over men and their submission and humiliation" as "a projection of the middle class's own hostility and envy" (1965, 115–16).

Lest this dichotomy between religions of the privileged and nonprivileged classes lead to an oversimplification, I wish to make one point. It is true that upper class religions tend to legitimize the established social order while lower class religions offer salvation or an agenda for moral reform. However, salvation religions, once established, possess alluring appeal (see Weber 1963), for they cater to basic needs resulting from human contingency, powerlessness, and scarcity of possessions (O'Dea 1966, 5–6). Since members of the privileged classes have not been able to eliminate death and other forms of suffering, they too may find other-worldly salvation irresistible. Meanwhile, they rarely abandon the religious beliefs that justify their privileged position.

THE PROBLEM OF SUFFERING.

Functional theory explains the origin, appeal, and role of religion for the individual and society in terms of three characteristics attributed to the human condition (see O'Dea 1966). *Contingency*, the first, refers to our dependence upon an environment over which we lack knowledge and control. Since many crucial events for human welfare—the very matters of life and death—defy complete comprehension, we cannot avoid a profound sense of "uncertainty." Moreover, we find ourselves, as a result, ultimately *powerless* in the face of our environment. If our ability to control the "conditions of life" is increasing—and this is contestable—it is nonetheless "inherently limited." Sociologist Thomas F. O'Dea called this sense of powerlessness the "impossibility context" and identified contingency as the "uncertainty context." Both refer to the inherent limitations of human existence.

Sigmund Freud defined the suffering resulting from our contingency and powerlessness as "privations." Suffering also results from the existence of human societies amid conditions of *scarcity*—the third characteristic of the human condition—which we either create or exacerbate. Every society allocates the material and nonmaterial resources at its disposal through social structures in accordance with cultural values. Unfortunately, most allocation systems leave some people with few rewards; and in all societies, from Freud's perspective, individuals are saddled with restrictions that inhibit the gratification of their needs. Both of these sources of frustration and suffering are human products. They are "deprivations" imposed by people upon people (Freud 1964).[1]

Religion emerges in these contexts by rendering the human situation meaningful. It does not, as I have indicated, eliminate contingency, powerlessness, and scarcity, but it does enable people to cope with these realities by infusing them with purpose and by making them comprehensible. This may be accomplished by projecting these very qualities onto the divine-human relationship itself. Thus Protestant Reformation and neo-orthodox theologies present sophisticated rationales for helplessness and the necessity of divine intervention—God is necessary and omnipotent while humans are contingent and helpless. By incorporating these very characteristics of the human condition into their theologies, Protestant neo-orthodox theologians render the human condition understandable while establishing a profound psychological need for the existence of God.

We have already encountered this phenomenon of projection in Marx's concept of the other-worldly religions of the poor. Freud also found the concept applicable in his analysis of humanity's effort to address contingency and

---

[1]While this is the most comprehensive, concise statement of his theory of religion, Freud's analyses of religious phenomena also appear in *Totem and Taboo*, *Moses and Monotheism*, and *Civilization and Its Discontents*. The latter, Freud's most insightful work from a sociological perspective, was written in response to critics of his *Future of an Illusion*.

powerlessness. Freud assumes that animism, the belief that the forces of nature or objects within the natural world have spirits, was born out of the human recognition of nature's power over us. Knowing that we can influence one another by attempting to understand the motives for our behavior, the "humanization" of nature enables us to deal with nature as though it were a fellow human being. No longer are we "helplessly paralyzed," for, as Freud noted, we can use the "same methods against these supermen outside that we employ in our society; we can try to adjure them, to appease them, to bribe them"—thereby robbing them of "part of their power" (1964, 22-23).

With this same process Freud explained the gods of civilization. They too were products of psychological projection. As children we suffered from contingency and powerlessness yet simultaneously felt the security of a mother and father who, it is hoped, loved, cared, and provided for us. In short, our parents appeared omniscient, omnipresent, and omnipotent. As we matured, we discovered that they also suffered and died, that they were not all-powerful and all-knowing. This existential crisis—the awareness that human existence itself is contingent and powerless—was resolved by regressing to our childhood solution of obtaining security through infallible parents. Now, however, we projected these qualities of omniscience, omnipotence, and omnipresence onto a heavenly father who would love and protect us. (It is, incidently, worth noting that the ultimate deity in a patriarchal civilization is a father, the primary symbol of authority in that society.) Thus to Freud, God is a projection of the parent-child relationship onto a reality transcending ordinary human experience. Religion is an expression of "wish-fulfillment" resulting from "infantile regression" (1964, 22–23).

So human beings, both Freud and Marx contend, created religious ideas by projecting their psychological states and social relations onto another existence in response to conditions of anxiety and suffering imposed by nature and society. If this failed to eliminate human contingency, powerlessness, and scarcity, it at least rendered them meaningful.

Perhaps our greatest social-psychological need is this discovery of meaning within our experience and environment. We do not merely experience birth, life, suffering, and death; we also try to understand them. Thus we employ a perspective—a belief system, an ideology, a model, a frame of reference—to comprehend our world. All of us use these, consciously or not, to interpret and understand our experiences and the objects within our environment.

Consider, for instance, a Christian fundamentalist who, eagerly awaiting the second coming of his Lord, is confronted with an earthquake in a distant land or with his own country's entrance into war. Both, he contends, are "signs of the times"—evidence that the "Day of the Lord is nigh at hand." Both are also evidence of human sinfulness and divine judgment, explainable by an eschatological perspective which, depending upon circumstances, is a basis for action or inaction. He may, as did a fundamentalist candidate for Congress during the Vietnam War, refuse to work for peace on the grounds that God had decreed the contemporary age "a time of war." This theological frame of reference, with its end-of-the-age motif, enabled him to explain war as an inevitable fact of life. Though war may result from human sin, it is not subject to human resolution.

How different is the frame of reference of a geologist who explains the earthquake in naturalistic terms or the perspectives of historians and social scientists who account for war as consequences of economic, political, geographical, social, cultural, ideological, and/or religious conflicts. Nevertheless, a frame of reference, providing the structural context through which these events are interpreted, underlies each approach.

In his classic study on *The Psychology of Social Movements*, Hadley Cantril describes such frames of reference. They may be "broad and inclusive," he writes,

> even though the assumptions upon which they are based have little factual data to support them. Nevertheless, to the individual, they may be just as adequate or just as helpful in interpreting his environment as the more verifiable frame of the sophisticate. If a person believes that God directs all the activities of nature and man, there will be few things to puzzle him; if he believes in the superiority of the white race, many of the questions which baffle the social scientist will for him be easily answered. No matter what the source of validity of a person's standards of judgment or frames of reference may be, experi-

ence will be meaningful to him so long as he can relate it appropriately to his particular mental context (1963, 57).

Not only do we require a frame of reference to make experience meaningful, but there is at least some indication that we possess a "need" to maintain a degree of cognitive consistency. Research by Leon Festinger and others working with "cognitive dissonance" theory indicates that when one holds cognitions (ideas, beliefs, and perceptions) that are recognized to be mutually inconsistent, he experiences tension or "dissonance" (see Festinger 1957; Festinger et al. 1956; "Self Justification" in Aronson 1972). Like the tension experienced with hunger, dissonance motivates behaviors that enable one to eliminate or reduce this tension. Consonance may be reestablished by dissonance reduction techniques in which an individual alters weaker cognitions or those most easily changed. Cognitions that are central to our self-concept or in which we have invested considerable material resources and psychological energies are highly resistent to change, even when they are disconfirmed.

In *When Prophecy Fails*, Festinger et al. apply the cognitive dissonance model to millenarian movements, with fascinating results. Religious movements that established dates for the end of the world and the return of Jesus did not die as these dates passed and the world remained intact. On the contrary, they tended to grow. Though an individual might abandon a belief upon disconfirmation, this was particularly difficult if he had sold all of his possessions to join the movement or had invested considerable psychological energy in it. Such dissonance was typically reduced by altering other cognitions or by adding new ones that enabled him to preserve his original commitment. So a group that has gathered in anticipation of the end of the world will be inclined to offer rationalizations accounting for the failure of the world to end instead of acknowledging their error. Perhaps God was so pleased with their faithfulness that he delayed destruction of the world. As others join the movement through increased proselyting, this provides consensual validation for the belief system. Cognitive dissonance thereby acts as an impetus for theological elaboration and more active involvement.[2]

Cognitive dissonance theory can also account for the psychological dynamics involved in Weber's observation that privileged people cannot simply live with their privileges but feel compelled to justify them. It also explains the psychological dynamics involved in French sociologist Emile Durkheim's analysis of anomie, or normlessness, a

---

[2]The Mormon concept of Zion as the location for the gathering of the faithful and the place for the Second Coming underwent similar elaboration. Having first located Zion in Jackson County, Missouri, the Saints were then forced to develop a theology for the redemption of Zion, subsequently relocating it in the "tops of the mountains," and eventually, with the de-emphasis on the "gathering," encouraging converts to remain in their native lands. Zion was then redefined as the "pure in heart," a state of mind instead of a geographical place. For a brief discussion of this phenomenon as a product of Mormon accommodation following the abandonment of polygamy, see my 1978 essay, "Mormonism in America and Canada."

condition in which cultural values and norms, which organize behavior and infuse life with meaning, disintegrate or break down. This is not a situation in which people choose to deviate from established norms but one in which they do not know what constitutes appropriate behavior. The norms themselves are unclear. Consequently, individuals find themselves without meaning and purpose for their behavior. The ambiguity and meaninglessness that follow from this social disintegration are intolerable, creating a state of tension, like cognitive dissonance, from which individuals seek to escape.

Durkheim described various responses to anomie that have been documented in subsequent research. The effort to escape the meaninglessness of life finds some engaged in excessive drinking, drug abuse, and even suicide (Durkheim 1951), while others, perhaps responding to less severe situations, act out deviant behavior patterns (see Merton 1957; Cloward 1959; O'Dea 1967). Affiliating with social movements or religious groups enables some to find new meaning and purpose—new norms and values—to replace the old and restructure their lives. Thomas O'Dea and Renato Poblete (1960, 18–36), in an interesting study of Catholic Puerto Rican immigrants to New York City, found them fleeing the anomie experienced in their new environment by embracing small pentecostal sects providing a greater sense of community and emphasis on personal identity.

So great is this need for meaning and so intolerable is ambiguity and dissonance that reports came from England at the outbreak of World War II indicating that the British had "regained their cheerfulness and enthusiasm" and were glad that the war had finally started (Cantril 1963, 62n10). Consistent with the subsequent research on cognitive dissonance, Hadley Cantril suggests that relief from indecision, even if it means intensive warfare, is more tolerable than a "tenuous peace" (ibid.).

THE CAUSES OF CRISES.

This example, that even the extreme condition of war is preferable to the ambiguity of an uneasy peace, underscores the importance of meaning in the human experience. Indeed, so important is meaning that crises may be defined in terms of the absence or inadequacy of meaning. A crisis may arise, as Cantril suggests, "when an individual is confronted by a chaotic external environment which he cannot interpret and which he wants to interpret. The more directly an individual's ego is involved, the more critical is the situation" (1963, 63). This is obviously a *personal* crisis. If it occurs at a collective level, as implied in the example above, and constitutes a threat to the security or existence of a group or society, then it is a *social* crisis. When it entails a significant breakdown in the normative order, as implied in the condition of anomie, it is a *cultural* crisis. As cultural or social crises are experienced by individuals, they become personal crises. (The significance of social and cultural crises for the development of theologies is discussed later in this chapter.)

The cultural crisis, which is my concern here, is frequently produced by events that render obsolete traditional frames of reference, by significant changes in social structures, and, finally, by the inadequacy of traditional norms and values. While it is likely that problems of meaning are as old as human consciousness, they took on a special poignancy with industrialization and the development of modern science. In his 1967 essay, "The Crisis in American Religious Consciousness," O'Dea compellingly argued that this century, including the 1950s and 1960s which constitute the formative period for the development of Mormon neo-orthodoxy, exacerbated the problem of meaning. In the United States, two world wars and a major depression raised serious questions about the liberal concept of "rational man," upon which our political system was founded, and about the positive assessment of human nature characteristic of Protestant liberalism and secular expressions of the "American spirit." These events, as argued in the following chapter, created a cultural crisis that led to the development of Protestant neo-orthodoxy with its opposite assumptions about human nature.

Many important changes in modern societies follow from social differentiation and secularization. While social differentiation refers to the process by which institutions become increasingly specialized in their functions and separated from one another (e.g., government, economy, family, and education), secularization refers to the removal of these spheres of society and culture from religious domination. A distinction between sacred and profane objects, institutions, and behaviors indicates the beginning of secularization; the further it proceeds, fewer elements of social and cultural life are considered sacred. Obviously a thoroughly secularized society would consider nothing sacred. Though some scholars deny this possibility by assuming a natural limit to secularization (see Swanson 1968, 801–34; Hadden 1987), others identify secularization with the modern cultural crisis (see O'Dea 1966; O'Dea 1967; Berger 1967; Westhues 1969). Peter Berger's emphasis on the "secularization of consciousness" underscores subjective as well as objective aspects in which peoples' lives are experienced without religious symbols:

> Secularization has posited an altogether novel situation for modern man. Probably for the first time in history, the religious legitimations of the world have lost their plausibility not only for a few intellectuals and other marginal individuals but for broad masses of entire societies. . . . In other words, there has arisen a problem of "meaningfulness" not only for such institutions as the state or for the economy but for the ordinary routines of everyday life. . . . There is good reason to think that it is also prominent in the minds of ordinary people not normally given to theoretical speculation and interested simply in solving the crises of their own lives (1967, 125).

This secularization of consciousness involves *desacralization* and the *rationalization of thought*. While the former implies the withholding of the emotional sensations associated with religious responses toward the sacred—the virtual elimination of the awe and mystery associated with religious experience and worship—the latter, involving cognition, implies an attitude relatively free from "emotional symbolism," in which the world is understood in terms of logical and empirically verifiable relationships (O'Dea 1966, 81).

Vast social change accompanies secularization. Not only is human consciousness desacralized, and institutions such as the family, economy, government, and education increasingly liberated from the influence of religion, but social statuses and roles that were traditionally linked to the social order through religious legitimations become obsolete. Thus priests and ministers find themselves increasingly displaced by secular counselors and therapists. As more people turn to psychiatrists, psychologists, and social workers for assistance with their personal lives, and to educators for moral guidance, the clergy become less important in society and lose both prestige and influence. People occupying clerical roles and those with a predominantly religious consciousness, who are likely to experience anxiety from this social dislocation, become likely candidates for the "generational dispossessed" (Bell 1963, 1–45).

If the dispossessed refers to all who lose power and prestige, then the generational dispossessed comprises all those who represent the traditional values and norms about which "people in all walks of life are less sure . . . than their fathers were" (Cantril 1963, 10–11). Confusion over the adequacy of "established ways" and the anomie emerging in the late 1950s and early 1960s were identified by several social scientists as major factors in the revival of religious fundamentalism and right wing politics (see ibid., 117; Bell 1963; Riesman 1963; Parsons 1963). Moreover, status anxiety—the conflict between subjective and objective status—experienced by many clerics created a cognitive crisis that led to a quest for new meaning. As Cantril suggests, an individual's need for meaning, a comprehensible interpretation of his situation, increases with his need to enhance his status (1963, 117). In other words, those clergy who find themselves fighting to maintain an eroding social position may be more apt to join and lead religious and political movements which provide a frame of reference by which their subjective status can be objectively realized.

This threat of secularization led many fundamentalists, both Catholic and Protestant, to subordinate old feuds and, according to Richard Hofstadter, "to unite in opposition to what they usually describe as 'godless' elements" (1963, 87n9). This united resistance to modernity, or secularization, is described by David Reisman:

> The rich and the poor fundamentalists have this much in common: they fear the way the world is going, at home or abroad; they resent those more cosmopolitan people who appear to understand the world less badly and who seem less ill at ease with all the different kinds of people who mingle in our big cities or at the United Nations. Moreover, whatever sectarian or doctrinal differences divide the discontented from each other in theological terms, all can agree on the gospel of Americanism (1963, 147–48).

In short, the threat of secularization, "still seen by most religious leaders in the West as a grave danger," remains "one of the most significant sources of conflict in the western world today" (O'Dea 1967, 90). It is associated with the destruction of religious frames of reference and a renewed intensity in the problem of meaning; the devaluation of religiously grounded social structures, statuses, and roles; and the obsolescence of traditional values and norms. When we experience these phenomena, either collectively or individually, we confront a profound critical situation.

TWO RESPONSES.

Although individuals and groups employ a variety of psychological mechanisms when threatened, I will identify only the two—irrationality and authoritarianism—that are relevant to my discussion. Both are natural responses, especially as initial reactions, to critical situations and are probably used by all of us at times. However, for the crisis theologian they are often intensified, and the theology typically becomes a religious or philosophical justification of their significance for humanity. As I argue in subsequent discussions of Protestant and Mormon neo-orthodoxy, both irrationality and an inordinate dependence on external authority are usually elevated to the status of virtues for a helpless humanity.

Irrationality, the denial of logical and objective criteria, often accompanies the breakdown of frames of reference, social roles and structures, and internalized norms and values. In fact, a well established generalization in the social sciences holds that individuals and groups do not

undergo such change without producing a high level of irrationality (Parsons 1963, 217–18). When this experience is
sufficiently traumatic, it threatens the basic structure of the
personality.

To individuals experiencing crises, the failure of their
frames of reference provides evidence that they are incapable of solving their own problems. Their normal intellectual and psychological processes for understanding the world
have failed. Being overwhelmed by their contingency and
powerlessness, such individuals are extremely anxious and
particularly sensitive to their inadequacies. Accordingly, they
abandon reason and seek security in something beyond
themselves. Thus irrationality can lead to authoritarianism—the second psychological response to crises.

Following the 1941 publication of Erich Fromm's
Escape From Freedom, an analysis of the development of the
authoritarianism of Nazi Germany, the authoritarian personality became a major theme in social science literature.[3]
My interest is not in delineating all of the traits comprising
the authoritarian personality, only the propensity for excessive submission to external authorities, such as government,

---

[3]Professional journals within both sociology and psychology have
devoted considerable attention to this problem. In addition to Fromm's
classic, two celebrated studies are those of Adorno (1950) and Rokeach
(1960). While Adorno concentrated on right wing authoritarianism,
Rokeach followed with an analysis of left wing authoritarianism. For
an interesting study of authoritarianism within Mormon society, see
Allen (1955).

church, or society. The identification with authority provides people with a frame of reference absolving them from
responsibility for their own actions. They may, consequently, escape from the ambiguity of the crisis through
the meaning provided by this authority. Such a resolution
is no longer dependent upon reason or other "human
frailties" but is assured by an external power much greater
than the individual.

THEOLOGICAL RESPONSES.

Different kinds of crises tend to give rise to different
kinds of theologies. Table 1, which differentiates social from
cultural and low from high intensity crises, assumes that
each cell contains a distinct type of crisis theology. While a
social crisis entails a threat to the movement or group itself,
a cultural crisis involves a challenge to the beliefs shared
by its adherents. A low intensity social crisis implies that
the group is persecuted and that there may be an attempt
by the host society to segregate or isolate it from others,
while a high intensity social crisis involves a threat to the
very survival of the movement or group. A low intensity
cultural crisis constitutes a challenge to certain beliefs of
the group, while a high intensity cultural crisis challenges
its basic assumptions and underlying frame of reference.
Indeed, the latter calls into question the legitimacy, the very
meaningfulness, of the belief system.

Messianic and apocalyptic theologies emerge out of
low intensity social crises in which the group experiences

CRISIS AND THEOLOGY

INTENSITY OF CRISIS.

LOCUS OF CRISIS.

	SOCIAL	CULTURAL
HIGH	MARTYROLOGY. ———	PESSIMISTIC THEOLOGIES. ——— (NEO-ORTHODOXY)
LOW	APOCALYPTICS. ———	APOLOGETICS. ———

persecution and social exclusion. Expectations and hopes for a more just society are usually vested in a messiah who will preside over the destruction of the existing society and introduce a new social order in which both the persecuted and the persecutors will receive their just rewards. The sudden destruction of society—the distinguishing characteristic of apocalyptic theology—is typically a prelude to the restoration or inauguration of a just society. While the Judeo-Christian tradition is pregnant with examples of apocalyptic literature (including, of course, the Book of Daniel and the Revelation of John), Marvin Harris has demonstrated that the phantom cargo cults of New Guinea, like the "cult of the vengeful messiah," were "born and continually re-created out of a struggle to overturn an exploitative system of political and economic colonialism" (1974, 133–75).

Although a low intensity social crisis entails serious persecution and exploitation, a high intensity social crisis involves the possible annihilation of the group. It gives rise to martyrological literature which is characterized by a promise of ultimate reward for individuals who are willing to die for the cause or group. Salo W. Barron and Joseph L. Blau note that with the crisis of the Maccabean revolt, beginning around 165 B.C., the Jewish community developed a significant martyrological literature (1954, xvi–xvii). Obviously the martyr's only hope of achieving his goal was to gain acceptance among his people or to receive a reward in another life. For religious movements with the concept of a hereafter where individual personality matters, the martyr is typically promised the highest possible form of salvation.

In the second century, the martyrology of the Christian community was so well developed that Ignatius, the bishop of Antioch, having been sentenced to death, importuned the Roman Christians to allow him this special opportunity of reaching God. Worried that influential Christians might again secure his release, he wrote, "I am writing to all the Churches to tell them all that I am, with all my heart, to die for god—if only you do not prevent it. I beseech you not to indulge your benevolence at the wrong time. Please let me be thrown to the wild beasts; through them I can reach God" (1947, 109).

The low intensity cultural crisis, which involves a challenge to particular beliefs, is characterized by apologetic theology (i.e., a literary exposition and defense of doctrine). It may result from a heretical challenge within the community or from external forces that cast doubt upon specific beliefs. With neither internal nor external challenges, the movement has little reason to clarify and defend doctrine. However, either threat is likely to produce apologetic literature.

For instance, second-century Christian clerics defended themselves against heresy within the church by arguing the position that authority was transferred to them by the early apostles. Thus the doctrine of "apostolic succession" justified the church's existence. Combined with the development of a canon of authoritative scriptures that were considered binding on the individual member and in which "truths" of the gospel could be preserved without alteration, the doctrine of apostolic succession protected the church from dissent.

A Mormon example of apologetics is the elaboration, until 1978, of a theology justifying denial of the priesthood to blacks during the racially conscious 1950s and 1960s. Efforts to connect the priesthood ban to Joseph Smith and to justify patterns of racial segregation within society characterized the writings of some Mormon officials and theologians (see White 1972; and especially Bush 1973). These efforts were obvious attempts to protect a specific belief and practice from the onslaught of external and internal criticism.

Neo-orthodox theology is a response to the high intensity cultural crisis. Since this crisis undermines a group's frame of reference and challenges its basic assumptions, the theological response requires a denial of fundamental human capacities. The primary cause of the high intensity cultural crisis is the secularization of culture which, as observed, undermines religious structures and encourages the rationalization of thought and the desacralization of human consciousness.

The neo-orthodox response is to deny the value of reason and autonomy and to celebrate human contingency and powerlessness. Since reason will not help us out of this predicament, humanity must rely upon some power greater than its own. Thus neo-orthodoxy identified the sensations

of contingency and powerlessness encountered during crises and rendered them dogmas of human nature; the psychological reactions of authoritarianism and irrationality
are also endowed with religious value and significance. The
crisis experience and the sensations accompanying it, in
short, are generalized to characterize the human condition
itself. They are embodied, as I will suggest in the next chapter, in neo-orthodoxy's fundamental proclamation of the
sovereignty of God, the depravity of human nature, and
the necessity of salvation by grace.[4]

---

[4]Protestant and Mormon neo-orthodox theologies contain elements
of other crisis theologies. Because of their historical legacies (i.e., the
persecution of Christian and Mormon communities), they share a
marked proclivity for apocalypticism. Similarly, the theological response
to high intensity social and cultural crises has elements of the theological responses from low intensity crises. Neo-orthodoxy should thus
contain considerable apologetics, while martyrology much apocalypticism. Moreover, there is no reason to assume that social and cultural
crises are mutually exclusive. They occur together and independently.

PROTESTANT NEO-ORTHODOXY.

CHAPTER 2.

At the hands of its most articulate, rigorous, and cele-brated theologians—Karl Barth, H. Emil Brunner, and Reinhold Niebuhr—Protestant neo-orthodoxy affirms divine sovereignty, human contingency, and the necessity of sal-vation by grace. To anyone even remotely familiar with the Reformation theologies of Luther and Calvin, neo-orthodoxy is hardly novel: it restates their thought within a contemporary context.

Neo-orthodoxy differs from Luther's and Calvin's theology, however, in its acceptance of a more modern world view and many of the conclusions of biblical scholarship. An orthodox fundamentalist has described the neo-orthodox theologian as an individual who is trying to be "at the same time a respectable intellectual (by believing evolution and destructive aspects of higher criticism) and an orthodox evangelical (by preaching the Gospel in the usual terms)" (Ryrie 1966, 17). Obviously, neo-orthodoxy is not the same as orthodoxy or fundamentalism.[1]

---

[1]Some scholars have abandoned the label neo-orthodoxy in favor of "Theology of the Word" as a better expression of the intent of neo-orthodox theologians. The reason is that neo-orthodoxy may imply the same literalistic approach to the Bible characterizing Reformation theology. I have chosen to retain neo-orthodoxy because it does embody

Even a cursory examination of the writings of Barth, Brunner, and Niebuhr reveals neo-orthodoxy's basic doctrine of the sovereignty of God. Barth, one of the most important theologians of this century, in *Dogmatics in Outline* (1959), a brief but excellent summary of his thought, describes three processes in which the sovereign God participates. First, God is the Creator. He has no origin, as Brunner suggests, for he is the origin of all that is. He "has no nature. He is not 'founded,' posited, based on anything save Himself. He posits Himself, and is therefore completely transparent to Himself" (Brunner 1939, 237-38). He has no beginning and will have no end. He simply is.

Through his "holy, overflowing love," God creates. He "puts something else, something different from Himself—namely the creature"—alongside himself, "without having need of it, in the power of His Almightiness" (Barth 1959, 39). His act of creation is *ex nihilo* (ibid., 55)—that is, it is a creation out of nothing. The *ex nihilo* creation is not one in which God takes some "nothing," as if nothing were something, and then creates something else. Rather, it is a creation where nothing, except God, exists. From the condition in which he alone exists, God originates his creation. Thus all existence outside of God is subject to God and

the spirit if not the letter of Reformation theology and because the label "Theology of the Word" would only be clear to professional scholars of religion. For those advocating a redefinition, see Mackintosh 1937, 263-72, and Macquarrie 1963, 319-21.

owes its being to him. It is his creature. To be a creature means to exist "in time and space, existence with a beginning and an end, existence that becomes in order to pass away again" (ibid.). Hence only God exists necessarily; only he could not *not* exist. All creation exists contingently and can only continue to be as God wills.

Although God is the Creator, his work is not finished with creation. He is also the Covenantor, having established a covenant between himself and humanity, his creation. Why God chose to do this is inconceivable since humans have always been unthankful and disobedient to him; from the very beginning, they have been sinners. But, in spite of human disobedience and ingratitude, God surrendered himself. He lent "Himself to become the God of a tiny, despised people in Asia Minor, Israel" (ibid., 39). He thereby originated a covenant between himself and human beings.

In addition to his work as Creator and as Covenantor, God is also the Redeemer, the invisible God made himself visible in the Word, Jesus Christ (John 1:14). God redeems human beings, restoring them to their appropriate relation to him, through the person of Jesus Christ, who is both God and man. Christ

> is at once the goal of the history of the nation Israel, and the beginning and starting point of the Church, and at the same time the revelation of the redemption, of the completion, of the whole. The whole work of God lives and moves in this one Person. He who says God in the

sense of Holy Scripture will necessarily have to say Jesus
Christ over and over again (Barth 1959, 39).

Moreover, according to Brunner, humans cannot participate in this act of redemption or salvation. For to share
in the act of salvation, to divide salvation between God
and human beings, is to make the latter co-partners with
God—to make them equal to God. Thereby a man or a
woman becomes a "fellow-god." "God is not Lord, not sovereign, but a partner; but this is mocking God. God proves
Himself to be the one God, that is, the true God, only
when He is sovereign, only when He proves himself to be
the one helper" (Brunner 1929, 62). In other words, God is
God only when he alone exists necessarily and is the Ground
of Being for all other existence.

Furthermore, neo-orthodox theologians generally
avoid describing God in terms of classical Christian absolutist categories. Attempting to limit their descriptions of
God—asserting that he is the "living God" of the Bible—
they, nonetheless, find it necessary to emphasize specific
attributes embodied in this traditional philosophical language. Thus Brunner speaks of God's "unconditional" and
"absolute" freedom which enables him to do as he wills
(1939, 262), and Barth describes God as "Almighty," beyond
limitation:

> He has this ability which is the foundation of reality, its
> determinant and its support: He has almightiness, that
> is, He has *everything*, He is the basic measure of every-
> thing real and everything possible. There is no reality
> which does not rest upon His as its possibility, no possi-

bility, no basis of reality, which would limit Him or be a hindrance to Him. He is able to do what He wills. Thus God's power might also be described as *freedom*. God is simply free. The concepts of eternity, omnipresence, infinity are included in it. He is mighty over everything that is possible in space and in time; He is the measure and the basis of time and space; He has no limit (1959, 46–47).

Even though Barth avoids the concept of omnipotence, his unlimited God is still clearly all-powerful:

> But God is not wholly or partly powerlessness, but He is real power. He is not one who can do nothing, nor is He one who cannot do everything, but He is distinguished from all other powers by being able to do what He wills to do. Where powerlessness comes into question, there we have not to do with God (ibid., 48–49).

We must recognize, however, that God is not simply "power in itself," according to Barth. To conceive of "power in itself" as God is to miss God "in the most terrible way." For God is almighty; not that "the Almighty" is God. The attempt to explain God's sovereignty in terms of "power in itself" is futile since "power in itself" is "Chaos, Evil, the Devil." "Power in itself" is bad; it is "the end of all things. The power of God, real power, is opposed to 'power in itself.' " Indeed, "power in itself" and God are "mutually exclusive" (ibid., 47–48). Through this distinction, Barth introduces a moral aspect—a sense of responsibility—into the concept of God's power.

Despite such descriptions evoking the imagery of classical Christianity, neo-orthodox theologians assert that God is nonconceptual. Barth writes,

> We must be clear that whatever we say of God in such human concepts can never be more than an indication of Him; no such concept can really conceive the nature of God. God is inconceivable. What is called God's goodness and God's holiness cannot be determined by any view that we have of goodness and holiness, but is determined from what God is (ibid., 46).

Barth argues that the Bible's message is that God lives, acts, works, etc.; it is not an attempt to define or to limit him through conceptualization.

Moreover, God is unprovable. To the neo-orthodox, God needs no proof. He is his own proof. He "proves Himself on every hand: Here I am, and since I am and live and act it is superfluous that I should be proved" (ibid., 38). Hence, rational speculations and philosophical arguments which attempt to prove God are vain. God is not to be proved through philosophical speculation and logic. He is his own proof.

Finally, in addition to the claim that God is inconceivable and unprovable, neo-orthodox crisis theologians assert that God is unsearchable. We cannot reach up to God, but God must reach down to us. No man or woman ever found God, for knowledge of God is acquired, not by years of effective searching, nor by sudden discovery on our part, but only by God willingly disclosing himself to us (ibid., 36–38). In fact, this is the essential difference between religion and revelation. Religion is the attempt of humans to reach God; revelation is the attempt of God to reach humanity. Religion is damned as a human enterprise and is considered, along with speculative philosophy, as an attempt to be like God. Revelation, on the other hand, is the only way to learn about God. Its first "work is to confound man's religious aspirations." Paul Tillich, in a perceptive critique of Barth's theology, discusses neo-orthodoxy's distinction between religion and revelation.

> There are many students of theology, especially in Continental Europe, who contrast divine revelation not only with philosophy but also with religion. For them religion and philosophy stand under the same condemnation, since both are attempts of man to be like God; both are demonic elevations of man above his creatureliness and finitude. And, of the two, religion is the more dangerous, because philosophy, at least in principle, can be restricted to the technical problems of logic and epistemology (1955, 2–3).

To summarize: the God of neo-orthodoxy is sovereign. Though beyond conceptualization, he is nonetheless described as absolute, using traditional theological categories. God is Creator, Covenantor, and Redeemer, and is unprovable, inconceivable, and unsearchable.

Perhaps more important is the neo-orthodox doctrine of human nature. For it is here that neo-orthodoxy differs most radically from liberalism. Since God created humans from a condition in which he alone existed, humans are totally his creation. The *ex nihilo* creation means that human existence, our very being, is completely dependent upon God who alone exists necessarily. To Emil Brunner, human contingency clearly means that "man *is* what he is because God has so made him. He has received his life, his existence, his peculiar being from God, precisely as thousands of animals have their characteristics from God" (1936, 46-47).

The implication of contingency is clear: we are God's property. In fact, Brunner asserts that the meaning of loving God—the admonition of the first of the ten commandments—is the recognition that we are God's property, not our own, and must act accordingly (ibid., 51). And contingency means not only that God may do with us as he wills, but that we owe all we are and have to him. Without God we are nothing. We have no knowledge, no morality, no happiness. In one of his polemics, Barth attacked liberal theology for de-emphasizing human contingency, thereby reducing the gulf separating God from humanity. "There is no question about it," he wrote, "here man was made great at the cost of God" (1960, 39).

Reinhold Niebuhr, who introduced neo-orthodox dogma into American theological circles with the publication of *Moral Man and Immoral Society*, assumed a less extreme position regarding human contingency. If Niebuhr shared Barth's belief that utopian schemes were doomed to fail because of their naively optimistic conception of human nature, he claimed that Barth's theology suffered from an excessive preoccupation with the gulf between the creature and the Creator. He wrote,

In the modern Barthian revival of Lutheran orthodoxy

the religious experience is practically exhausted in the sense of contrition. The emphasis on the difference between the holiness of God and the sinfulness of man is so absolute that man is convicted, not of any particular breeches against the life of the human community, but of being human and not divine (1932, 68).

Protestant liberalism may have ignored human contingency and obliterated the gulf between God and humanity, but the Barthian revolution erred in the opposite direction. Its excesses were equally repudiated with Niebuhr's reminder of the "paradoxical nature of man," assuring that he is "both a child of God and a sinner" (Niebuhr 1963, 147). (Incidently, contingency was reaffirmed in Niebuhr's argument that democracy functions best when it rests on a conception of human limitation and not merely on rationality [1944, xv].)

So the human condition is also characterized by sinfulness. Brunner, for instance, described humanity as absolutely helpless because "we are sinners, not merely now and then but, so far as we are concerned, sinners always, hopeless sinners" (1929, 74). And Barth, in his commentary on Romans 5, writes, "So we were weak, sinners, godless, and enemies, always Adam in us and ourselves in Adam" (1962, 40). But what is this sin? And what does it mean to be a sinner?

With important qualifications, neo-orthodoxy reaffirms the Reformation concept of original sin (see Niebuhr 1944, 16–17). To Luther and Calvin, the human predicament is a condition or state of sin. Sin is not a specific act;

specific acts are the fruits of sin. Though they follow naturally from the condition of human sinfulness, the fruits of
sin must not be confused with sin itself. Adultery, for
instance, is not sin but rather a consequence, or product,
of human sinfulness. Sin is the condition from which we
all act. That is, everything that humans do is sin because
all men and women are in a state of sin. They are inherently and irrevocably sinners.

Niebuhr laments modern society's rejection of original sin—the "sober and true view of the human situation"—
because it makes "an important contribution to any social
and political theory" (ibid.). However, neither he, Barth,
nor Brunner accepts the classical Christian explanation for
the origin of the human predicament. In other words, they
reject the story of Adam as a factual account of creation
and qualify their conception of original sin.

In order to avoid the criticisms leveled against the
traditional doctrine, Brunner defines sin as an act rather
than a state. Through an impressive argument, he concludes
that the whole person is a sinner. However, to be a sinner
is not to be equated with "being a sinner" in the sense of a
child "being blue-eyed" or a dog "being a mammal," for
these are static categories. Humans are persons, and a person is a "being-in-decision." He is an actor, and whenever
he acts, he sins (Brunner 1939, 148).

Indeed, by attempting to become independent from
God, humanity is in an act of rebellion against God. The
whole person is set at odds with God. To be a person, for

Brunner, is to be an actor acting against God. He concludes his argument with a discussion of Luther's conception of sin: "To him the doctrine of Original Sin is the means provided by tradition to visualize this in his mind. The method of expression is often questionable, but the truth which he is trying to express, namely, that the whole person is sinful, is indeed the whole point at issue. The Bible says this, and nothing else" (ibid., 150).

On the other hand, sin is only part of the story. Humans are also children of God. Thus Niebuhr writes:

> "The simplicity of the gospel" means the affirmation of the basic paradox of human existence: the fact, namely, that man is both a child of God and a sinner, that the same majestic freedom which enables man to be creative also gives him the capacity, and perhaps the inclination, to do evil, which means usually, perversely to make himself the center of every value scheme. There is a mystery about the human capacity for good and the human inclination to evil which has been explicated in the Biblical faith but obscured in even the profoundest philosophies (1963, 147).

This dual nature is also apparent in the theologies of Barth and Brunner. In his exegesis of Romans 5, *Christ and Adam*, Barth discusses the human relationship to Christ and Adam. Even sinful human nature is not to be found in its affinity to Adam but in the revelation of Jesus Christ. Only through Christ, who is both the son of God and of man, can we understand human nature. Christ was above humanity. Through him humankind transcends the duality of its nature.

To Emil Brunner the fact that we were created in the image of God and yet oppose him establishes a contradiction in human nature. He writes:

> Let us not quibble about words. The point at issue is this: the state of mind which reaches its nadir in despair is the contradiction between man's "true" and his "actual" nature, between his Divine destiny in Creation and his self-determination in actual experience, and it is this conflict which not only runs right through human life as a whole, but is also somehow felt by all men, even if dimly and obscurely, as a sense of hopeless division, of being "torn in two." Even the happy and placid person is not so happy and placid as he thinks, or makes other people think, he is. Even he perceives, though dimly, that his life is torn, that he is inwardly bleeding from an unhealed wound at the centre of his personality, his heart. Even he observes that he cannot "square" his own ideal of life and his actual life-experience, that things are out of proportion, the symmetry has been disturbed, "something has gone wrong" (1939, 201).

Even though the contradiction eventually may be resolved, Brunner at least views this life in extremely pessimistic terms. History, he explains,

> is always, without the slightest exception, the history of sinful man. If man rises to higher levels of intellectual or cultural life, so does sin. It follows him like his shadow. He cannot get rid of it wherever he may go. For he takes it with him; in fact we ought not to say "it" because the "it" is himself. He is the sinner, and wherever he goes and whatever he does, he goes and does as a sinner (1929, 101).

Undoubtedly this depravity and contingency mean that humanity is lost. Criticizing Schleiermacher for a naively optimistic conception of human nature, Barth declares:

> With all due respect to the genius shown in his work, I can *not* consider Schleiermacher a good teacher in the realm of theology because, so far as I can see, he is disastrously dim-sighted in regard to the fact that man as man is not only in *need* but beyond all hope of saving himself; that the whole of so-called religion, and not least the Christian religion, *shares* in this need; and that one can *not* speak of God simply by speaking of man in a loud voice (1957, 195–96).

Neo-orthodoxy's third fundamental tenet is hereby revealed: the necessity of salvation by grace. If we were not completely helpless and powerless—totally dependent upon forces outside ourselves—perhaps we could help save ourselves. However, says Brunner, "if the contradiction consists in man's antagonism toward God, then a reconciliation on the part of man is out of the question. And, I say it advisedly, not merely a complete, but even a partial, clearing up of the contradiction on man's part is thus excluded" (1929, 56).

Though helpless, powerless, and undeserving, humanity still has hope since the "sin of Adam is not comparable with the grace of Christ" (Barth 1962, 49). If destroyed through sin, human nature is restored through grace. Grace "has the last word about the true nature of man" (ibid., 56). Moreover, grace is entirely divine. It is a gift from God who alone is able to restore human nature. God initiates grace, he acts, he reaches toward humanity. "God has mercy on men; He even comes to those who do not come to Him; He troubles Himself about them, follows after them like a good shepherd after his erring sheep" (Brunner 1936, 8).

Through grace we are elected, saved, restored to our divine nature, "raised up from eternal death to attain the glorious liberty of the children of God" (Barth, in Casalis 1963, 102–103). We know that we are saved without our own effort and only by the loving, gracious act of God. In his most important work, *Man in Revolt*, Brunner summarizes God's act of election and then proceeds to point out that redemption is not completed in this life.

> The manner in which the contradiction is overcome in faith is: the Atonement. Atonement means: the rediscovery of man's original position, his restored position in God. This status is expressed as a condition or state; and only the status, not the state, is completed. The knight has been dubbed knight, his patent of nobility has been issued, but the knight is still, in his condition, a "commoner," his nobility has not yet permeated his whole nature; redemption is not to be separated from atonement, it is true, but it is not yet completed. Man still awaits the consummation of Redemption; this consummation would mean the transition from faith to sight, complete deliverance from this "body of death," from all that is contradictory in our present state, from that participation in the curse which even the man who has been reconciled to God still bears; for as a member of the human race he shares in the sin of all. Redemption therefore can only be consummated on the other side of this earthly existence (1939, 491).

Neo-orthodoxy offers hope ultimately but not in this life. A sovereign God is necessary to resolve the contradiction of human depravity through salvation by divine grace. Thus neo-orthodoxy offers its explanation and resolution of the human predicament.

SOCIAL CRISES

Significant social factors shaped the origin and development of Protestant neo-orthodox theology. Intellectual crises within the Christian community, as well as social and cultural crises of twentieth century western civilization, were of special importance.

Liberalism, neo-orthodoxy's immediate theological predecessor, also resulted from complex social forces. Both the Age of Reason and the Enlightenment—with their attendant increase in knowledge, emphasis on reason, and faith in human potential—produced a profound spirit of optimism which the course of Western history seemed to enhance with its

> relative peace; rapid industrialization and growth of trade; a rising standard of living; political liberalism and steps toward more democratic structures of government; economic theories of a "harmony of interests"; the Romantic movement; the use of the idea of evolution in the interpretation of the course of history; and the new-found confidence in the scientific method. Man's age-long struggle against nature seemed almost ended. The final victory was not yet here, but the means for achieving it were, and the time when men could live in harmony and free from physical want was just around the corner (Dillenberger and Welch 1954, 214).

These conditions encouraged a unique reinterpretation of traditional Christianity. Protestant liberalism was not, as some suppose, a decline in religious faith. On the contrary, it reflected a resurgence of religious vitality that was simply redirected. For the first time in its history, a significant Protestant movement focused upon social rather than individual life. This religious enthusiasm, with its grand optimism, became an integral part of the new social gospel.

However, the implications for traditional Christianity were not limited to the social gospel's emphasis on action. Theology too was transformed. The transcendent God of classical Christianity fell before an immanent God who, in the expression of William James, actively works with human beings to make the world a better place in which to live. God was no longer separate from his creation, he was now a personal God *within* the world. The radical discontinuity implied in the classical Christian distinction between the natural and supernatural made little sense to Protestant liberals whose emphasis on continuity bridged the divine/human gulf. Problems of human contingency, finitude, and creaturelessness received minor attention.

Not only was this disregard for contingency consistent with favorable social conditions reflecting human supremacy over the environment, but also with liberalism's doctrine of human nature. "Personality was hailed as the supreme value" (ibid., 222). Liberalism stressed the ideal person, not the actual person; the potentialities of people, not their failures; human dignity, not human depravity.

In contrast to the orthodox Christian doctrine of

the inherent evilness of humanity, liberalism boldly proclaimed the basic goodness of human nature. It rejected
the doctrine of original sin and the fall of man. Liberal theology did not deny the reality of sin, as some have asserted,
but it redefined it. Sin was no longer conceived of as a condition from which human action issues. Instead, it was identified with the action itself. In other words, people sin when
they violate their dignity or the dignity of others; but when
they develop the good in themselves or in others, this is
not only good but it reveals basic human nature. Never
claiming that humans were perfect, liberalism nonetheless
assumed their perfectibility.

Compare p. 36

From the doctrines of an immanent God and the
perfectibility of humanity, liberalism did not need a savior
in the orthodox Christian sense. Indeed, people were not
in a predicament from which they needed salvation. Furthermore, they possessed the power within themselves to
change conditions—the power, if you will, to save themselves.

Yet this does not imply that liberal theology left no
place for Jesus. On the contrary, the importance of Jesus is
found in his exemplary moral life. Through Jesus we learn
the good life and the way to God. It is not through an
atonement that humankind is reconciled with God, nor
through divine grace where some are elected to salvation,
but rather through the moral and natural perfection of the
individual personality.

Jesus is the liberals' savior; but, since the meaning

of salvation is different for the liberal, so is the role of a
savior. If salvation came for classical and neo-orthodox
Christians through the *death* of Christ, it came for liberals
through the *life* of Jesus.

Since scholars typically refer to war and depression
as the crises giving rise to neo-orthodoxy, this discussion of
liberal theology is necessary to provide a more complete
context for the emergence of neo-orthodox theology. In the
early years of the twentieth century, Christianity confronted
an internal, profoundly significant crisis, which the inordinate attention to war and depression obscures. The Christian community was seriously divided between classical and
liberal theology, and the social milieu tended to favor liberalism in its competition with traditional orthodoxy. There
was, as Emil Brunner would later suggest, a crisis within
Christianity.

In the Swander Lectures of 1928, subsequently published as *The Theology of Crisis*, Brunner identified this crisis as the rapid dissolution of Protestant theology. The cause,
of course, was liberalism. Its tolerance of non-Christian views
was matched only by its tentativeness toward Christian
beliefs, both of which were unpardonable. The absolutes of
Christianity were gone. If there was anything absolute in
liberalism, Brunner argued, it was absolute uncertainty
(1929, 8). The liberals had betrayed Christianity.

Moreover, liberalism had created another problem.
Theology and even belief became secondary to practical
religion. Morals and ethics were the essence of the gospel,

and the profession of belief and faith was subordinate to it. To Brunner this decay of "theological consciousness" portended the "complete decomposition" of Christianity:

> Christianity is either faith in the revelation of God in Jesus Christ or it is nothing. From this faith it derives its name, and has its peculiar content, its claim, its history. With it Christianity stands or falls. In the course of the last two centuries—or, in the case of America, the last three decades—a process of transubstantiation has gone on which has resulted in something utterly distinct from Christian faith and theology (ibid., 3–4).

Brunner's criticism of liberalism was destined to become popular. Liberalism, to the neo-orthodox, was merely a secular substitute for the Christian gospel. It denied the fundamental doctrines of Christianity and destroyed both the purpose and potency of the gospel. In 1934, Reinhold Niebuhr wrote:

> The liberal culture of modernity is defective in both religious profundity and political sagacity. . . . Liberalism understands neither the heights to which religious life may rise nor the depths to which it might sink. . . . It is quite unable to give guidance to a confused generation which faces the disintegration of a social system and the task of building a new one (1934, 14).

Three years later, his brother, H. Richard Niebuhr, accused liberalism of impotence for preaching that "a God without wrath brought men without sin into a kingdom without judgment through the ministrations of a Christ without a cross" (in Dillenberger and Welch 1954, 185).

To the neo-orthodox theologians, liberalism promised eventually to destroy Christianity. Indeed, Brunner was convinced that the liberals threatened Western civilization itself. "An age which has lost its faith in an absolute has lost everything. It must perish; it has not vitality left to pass the crisis; its end can only be—the end" (Brunner 1929, 8). The condition of Christianity was summarized in Brunner's paraphrase of scripture: "If ever the art of pouring new wine into old skins was successfully practiced, modern theology may claim the prize" (ibid., 6).

Excellent point.

The "complete decomposition" of Christian theology, which neo-orthodox theologians anticipated, would follow from *desacralization* and the *rationalization of thought* accompanying the secularization process described in the previous chapter. Liberalism's betrayal was implicated in both. Liberalism helped to dismantle the Christ—Christianity's ultimate object of worship. Christ became Jesus the teacher and exemplar. And the quest for the historical Jesus, a pursuit encouraged by liberals, resulted in further skepticism regarding his peculiar claim to divinity.

The rationalization of thought appeared in accepting the results of biblical criticism, the encouragement of biblical research, and the participation by liberals as biblical scholars. The question of Jesus' historicity was addressed through the eyes of an "objective" historian rather than the "emotional needs" of an orthodox theologian. Using logical and empirical methods in his research, the liberal scholar abandoned much of the biblical account of Jesus. He also rejected those other portions of the Bible found to be mythical. The Christ of orthodoxy appeared more like the spiritual God of the Docitists, who only seemed to suffer and die on the cross, than the actual Jesus of the synoptics. Accordingly, the liberals either rejected or radically reinterpreted Jesus' significance for humanity. The transformation of Christian theology into secular morality—of Christ on the cross into Jesus the moral teacher—confirmed the worst suspicions of neo-orthodox theologians.

If this internal crisis was not sufficient to explain the rise of Protestant neo-orthodoxy, it accounts for the revival of orthodoxy expressed in Protestant fundamentalism. Fundamentalism is primarily a reaction to secularization, especially the "modernity" embraced by liberalism. Fundamentalism assumed a rigid posture against science and its implications for the biblical world view. Adopting a biblical literalism that enabled them to reject both evolutionary explanations for the origin of the human species and the conclusions of biblical scholarship, the fundamentalists needed only this challenge from the liberal theologians to appear as the guardians of traditional Christianity.

Though sensitive to the internal crisis produced by science and secularism, other theologians required greater disenchantment to find the assumptions of classical theology appealing. Though perhaps more skeptical, neo-orthodox theologians, like the liberals, accepted modern science and its implications for the biblical world view. Like the liberals, they were professionally trained and well educated. In fact, neo-orthodox theologians, often educated as liberals, found themselves rebelling only as the social conditions supporting liberalism crumbled. The failure of "rational men" to resolve international conflicts at the conference table prior to World War I demonstrated the paucity of liberalism's assumptions about human nature. Technological advances offering hope for a better society were as easily employed for destruction as for amelioration. Science, humankind's newest savior, now revealed itself as the "destroying angel." Humanity no longer seemed as good, its potential as great, or its perfectibility as possible. "It is our acquaintance not with savage and unmoral man," Barth would remind us, "so much as with moral man that makes us none too proud of his achievements" (1957, 147).

For European theologians, World War I was sufficient reason to reject the frame of reference of Protestant liberalism. Defeated and humiliated, Germany especially provided rich soil for pessimistic philosophy and theology. As H. Richard Niebuhr wrote, in a preface to the translation of Paul Tillich's *The Religious Situation*,

> The crisis is naturally more acute and the problems are more sharply defined in Germany than elsewhere, not only because the German temper runs to sharp antitheses and exclusive definitions but also because that country has been visited by a severer fate in our time than the other countries of the West have been (1932, 22–23).

Neo-orthodoxy emerged out of the social crises of post-World War I Germany, social conditions antithetical to those sustaining liberalism. So Karl Barth and Emil Brunner began their labors in fertile soil.

Despite the ravages of World War I, Americans generally remained optimistic. Though they had been embroiled in a global war, it was "a war to make the world safe for democracy." Understood from the frame of reference of American liberalism, World War I may have been an unfortunate regression in human progress, but it was hardly sufficient to support Luther's and Calvin's bleak concept of human nature. The assumptions of Protestant liberalism were still too much a part of American life.

However, the advent of economic depression and burgeoning international tensions rendered even the Americans receptive to Reinhold Niebuhr's forceful presentation of neo-orthodoxy. In 1932, Niebuhr published *Moral Man and Immoral Society*, in which he wrote:

> The breadth and depth of the world depression have, moreover, tempted others beside proletarians to express a temper of catastrophism. If they do not share the proletarian hope, that salvation will come out of catastrophe, they are at least inclined to question the possibility of avoiding catastrophe by methods of gradual social change, and await the revolution in the ambivalence of hope and fear (1932, 169).

The inhumanity of capitalism (Barth 1957, 18) and the atrocities of World War II—with the brutal execution of six million Jews, not to mention the wholesale slaughter of

"Humanity" once Platonism (humanity) is perverse again rather than individual humans! is a reactionary influence!

millions of others—seemed to provide empirical confirmation of neo-orthodoxy's central thesis that humans are inherently sinners. Indeed, the post-war period, with the development of the cold war, underscored the propensity of using human intelligence, science, and technology for destructive ends. Unparalleled technological and scientific advances left the world in a still more precarious position. It is far from clear that social and political conditions have improved. A "balance of terror," in which opposing sides still possess the capacity to annihilate each other, undergirds the uneasy peace of humanity resting on the brink of Armageddon. Even in the nuclear age, "civilized men" seem no more capable of resolving their differences at the conference table than were their ancestors centuries ago.

Thus, the crisis of the nuclear age, with the constant threat of the extinction of all life, renders the neo-orthodox concept of human nature plausible. The appeal of neo-orthodoxy follows from the fact that modern humanity lives continually on the brink of a critical situation.

PSYCHOLOGICAL AND THEOLOGICAL RESPONSES

Cultural crises are often preconditions for religious conversion because they invalidate traditional and accepted frames of orientation. Casting doubt upon logical and psychological methods of coping with the world, they thrust people into a confrontation with their inadequacy, contingency, and powerlessness. This recognition of helplessness is often construed as a revelation of God's sovereignty, human contingency, and the necessity of salvation. The latter, under these conditions, typically comes as a gracious gift from a sovereign God rather than from within the individual.

Such was the experience of the neo-orthodox theologian. The crises described above revealed human contingency, sinfulness, and powerlessness. A critical situation discloses the human predicament; it demonstrates human sinfulness (see Brunner 1939, 489). This is the first step in accepting the need for grace. Indeed, the crisis experience itself is a religious experience to the neo-orthodox; for it discloses fundamental human nature—alienation, or a total separation from God—along with humanity's unwillingness to admit perversity, and a sinister effort to place itself at the center of everything. Brunner described the crisis situation as the "most important point of contact for the Gospel message." As a basis for conversion, the individual feels

> completely passive; he has no power over his feeling, the disharmony of his existence comes out in his feeling, against his will, while in thought and will, to some extent at least, he is able to go beyond himself. His feeling as a whole is the total balance of his existence which is drawn up and presented to him without his will; no skillful intellectual speculation and no deliberate positing of an end for his will can alter this. This unstilled longing for life, this negative balance of life, is therefore in the Bible everywhere the most important point of contact for the gospel message: "If any man thirst let him come unto Me and drink" (ibid., 234).

Though he had given up preaching sometime before his death, Barth still preached to inmates at a major prison in Basel (Casalis 1963, 89–93). There he could preach the fundamentals of the gospel—divine forgiveness, deliverance, and grace—to a "captive" audience. Incarceration stripped people of the "usual masks" they wear and left the prisoner in a unique position to recognize his predicament. The prison provided the perfect analogy with the human predicament in which everyone is a prisoner in need of deliverance. The prison constituted a ready-made critical situation, and Barth's message of human contingency and depravity resonated with the realities of prison life. Aware of their own predicament, their dependency and helplessness, the prisoners could respond readily to the message of divine grace and deliverance.

In no sense was Barth oblivious to the relationship between world conditions and the renewal of Christian vitality. "I am sure," he wrote, "that the course of events has aroused in many hunger and thirst for the Word of God, and that a great hour has arrived for the Church" (1959, 33).

The crisis experience, with the realization of helplessness, often causes people to doubt their own powers. Reason, for instance, is no longer trusted, and a denial of its efficacy can lead to a celebration of nonrationality. The overwhelming sense of the inadequacy of the intellect is often enshrined in the theology of neo-orthodoxy. Thus Brunner suggests that revelation occurs in a way that emphasizes God's "inaccessibility to our thought and imagination" (1936, 11–16). The major problem with theology is its propensity to systemization, that is, to subject revelation to reason. However, human reason cannot withstand the "a-logical" teachings of the Gospel. "We should leave the Scripture as it is, unsystematic, in all its parts; otherwise we pervert its message" (ibid., 33). Apparently a primary role of revelation is to baffle the intellect so that the individual will be responsive to divine will. This failure of reason is a precise revelation emerging out of the critical situation.

In spite of this attack on the intellect, some neo-orthodox theologians claim that they are not irrational (see Brunner 1939, 243–44). If reason is held within proper bounds, it can be good. But reason must be understood from the point of view of God, not God from the point of view of reason. "Reason is right wherever it listens to the Word of God, and does not think that it is able to proclaim divine truth itself" (ibid.). Barth identifies some of the limitations of reason: "Reason sees the small and the larger but not the large. It sees the preliminary but not the final, the derived but not the original, the complex but not the simple. It sees what is human but not what is divine" (1957, 9). In disciplines like the formal sciences and mathematics, Brunner conceded, the influence of sin is minimal; so it would be meaningless to speak of a Christian mathematics. Any area addressing humanity, however, is so tainted with the influence of sin that reasoning cannot be trusted (Macquarrie 1963, 324–27).

The denial of the efficacy of reason can lead neo-orthodox theologians to cast serious dispersions on doubt. When we doubt, we are in bondage:

> We are not yet Christians. For to doubt eternal life is to dismiss the promises of God, to be disobedient to the Word of God, to put our trust in our own understanding and senses. God's Word is not sufficient guarantee, we want something more certain. But this desire for something more certain than God's Word *is* crass, naked doubt; crass, naked paganism; crass, naked Godlessness (Brunner 1936, 144–45).

Reason causes doubt, destroys faith, and provides "pallid and academic substitutes for the loss of faith," which "from the very outset contain the seeds of doubt." Only that faith that realizes the "misunderstanding of reason within itself" can withstand doubt—"faith which knows that reason is derived from the Word of God" (Brunner 1939, 199–200). This faith alone knows the inadequacy of reason and the necessity of revelation to save humanity from this cultural crisis.

The neo-orthodox religious experience does not end with the realization that we are lost sinners who cannot rely upon our inadequate mental faculties. The most important aspect of the neo-orthodox revelation is, in fact, the "good news" that God wants to save humankind—that God wants to reach down, take our hand, and lift us out of our predicament. While God's goodness and mercy are evident in his willingness to save us, so is the necessity of our reliance on an agent outside ourselves. This preoccupation with

"grace" and denial of human possibilities for the amelioration of adverse conditions suggest an underlying
authoritarianism. Humanity is incapable of saving itself in
time or eternity. Only a transcendent God, a wholly other,
can perform such a feat. Without coming to God, our fate
is sealed. Remember Brunner's warning that an "age which
has lost its faith in an absolute has lost everything. It must
perish; it has no vitality left to pass the crisis; its end can
only be—the end" (1929, 8).

So it is the critical situation that reveals the human
predicament. The contingency, powerlessness, nonrationality, and authoritarianism associated with the crisis situation, when people are especially sensitive to their inadequacies, become elements of theology. The neo-orthodox
theologian projects these psychological phenomena onto
human nature itself, and they become the foundation of
the basic doctrines—divine sovereignty, human depravity,
and salvation by grace—of Protestant neo-orthodoxy.

TRADITIONAL MORMON THEOLOGY.

CHAPTER 3.

It was a turbulent era in American history that gave birth to Mormonism (see O'Dea 1957, 1–21; Brodie 1945; Bushman 1984). On the one hand, it was a time of "enlightenment" and skepticism. Basic assumptions of Reformation Christianity were subjected to vigorous criticism. The depraved, helpless human creature of Luther and Calvin seemed inconsistent with the rationality assumed by the American Constitution and the national consciousness of the new nation. Optimism generated from an increasing standard of living, opportunity provided by a limitless frontier, success of democratic forms of government, the extension of political and economic freedom, and increased confidence in reason, scientific method, and education—which combined to produce Protestant liberalism—profoundly influenced early Mormonism.

This age, on the other hand, was also one of deep religious "emotionalism," exaggerated supernaturalism, and folk magic (see Quinn 1987). In no sense was Mormonism oblivious to these forces. On the contrary, it was, at least partially, a product of the "Burned-Over District"—a label attached to western New York during the early 1800s because of the intensity of its revivalism (see Cross 1950). The emotional fervor of its conversions, the imminence of

apocalyptic expectations, and a reliance upon the supernatural sired numerous religious movements, of which Mormonism was the most successful.

Experiencing cross-pressures from these environmental forces, some movements turned toward a position
that would later come to be known as fundamentalism, while
others turned toward liberalism. Mormonism eventually did
both. It retained a biblical literalism as the means of express-
ing its new liberal theology. In the words of Sterling M.
McMurrin, a perceptive analyst of Mormon theology,
Mormonism is ''a unique and uneasy union of nineteenth-
century liberalism with fourth-century Christian fundamentalism'' (1965, 113).

This dual heritage obscures Mormonism's liberalism
so that Mormons and non-Mormons alike typically misun-
derstand some of the more subtle implications of Mormon
theology. Due to a commitment to biblical literalism, Mormonism is frequently considered another expression of fundamentalist Christianity. However, this notion—widespread
though it may be—fails to account for the basic liberal doctrines which oppose the central tenets of Christian orthodoxy. Moreover, the metaphysics assumed in Mormon
thought guarantees theological deviation from traditional
Christianity. By discussing its basic doctrines of God, human
nature, and salvation, the liberal character of traditional
Mormon theology will hopefully become apparent.

GOD

Mormons typically assume that their theology departs most significantly from classical Christianity in its doctrine that God is a person with a tangible body. While this has implications for divine omnipresence, it is hardly the most radical difference between the Mormon and traditional Christian notions of God. On the contrary, the finite character of God, which permeates traditional Mormon thought, is a much bolder denial of Christian orthodoxy.

A finite God follows logically from Mormon metaphysics. Since God is not the only entity existing necessarily, he is not the creator of all that is. In other words, he does not bring nonexistent entities into being; he organizes extant materials into new forms. The Mormon God is analogous to a builder and an architect rather than to a creator. This is not to say that Mormons do not speak of God as a creator, but that the Mormon concept of creation does not involve God creating the universe "out of nothing." He takes existing matter from which he "organizes," "prepares," and "forms" the objects of the universe. He creates the world the same way a builder creates a building. Using existing materials, he erects a structure.

In the Book of Abraham (3:24, in PGP), a Mormon revelation of the Creation, the Son of God is depicted as saying to a group of pre-existent spirits: "We will go down

for there is space there, and we will take these materials,
and we will make an earth whereupon these [the pre-existent
spirits of all human beings to inhabit the earth] may dwell."
The gods, throughout the remainder of this account,
"organize" the earth, "prepare" the waters, and "form"
man. They never "create" anything. Though Mormon literature abounds in references to the Creation, it is not to
the *ex nihilo* creation of classical Christianity.

In fact, Mormonism finds the *ex nihilo* creation
absurd. Even so, the typical Mormon argument miscon-
strues the meaning and significance of this doctrine for traditional Christianity (see Roberts 1893, 317; cf. McMurrin
1965, 19–48). Most Mormon literature assumes that an *ex
nihilo* creation is a creation from nothing in that nothing is
presumed to be something (see J. Smith 1938, 350–51; see
also Larson 1978; Cannon 1978; Hale 1978; Hale 1983).
But to those familiar with traditional Christian theology,
the *ex nihilo* creation has a different meaning. Its value
involves a distinction between necessary and contingent
being. God alone exists necessarily. He cannot not exist.
All else—space, time, heaven, earth, human beings, etc.—
owes its very existence to him. Without him, it could not
exist; and at his will, it can be destroyed. To be contingent
means to have one's existence dependent upon something
else. Thus the real meaning of the *ex nihilo* creation is that
the creature is contingent upon the creator. All creation
owes its existence to the creator and without his sustaining
support will cease to exist. The important point, then, is

not that God created the world out of nothing, but that everything that exists is completely dependent upon him for its being. Without God, it cannot exist.

If the meaning of the *ex nihilo* creation is frequently misunderstood by Mormons, it nonetheless profoundly contradicts fundamental tenets of Mormon theology when understood correctly. Mormonism denies that God alone has necessary being. For Mormon metaphysics assumes a pluralistic materialism in which all matter—including spirit, since even it is conceived of as more pure and refined matter—exists necessarily. A Mormon revelation proclaims that "the elements are eternal" (D&C 93:33), and Joseph Smith, in a polemic against the *ex nihilo* creation, declared that to create

> means to organize; the same as a man would organize materials and build a ship. Hence, we infer that God had materials to organize the world out of chaos—chaotic matter, which is element, and in which dwells all the glory. Element had an existence from the time he had. The pure principles of element are principles which can never be destroyed; they may be organized and reorganized, but not destroyed. They had no beginning, and can have no end (1938, 350–52).

This metaphysical materialism not only assumes that God and the elements exist necessarily, but so do space and time. In contrast, traditional Christian orthodoxy maintains that space and time, along with everything else except God, exist only because God created them. They would not be if God had not willed their existence.

To most Mormons God exists within time and space; he is not their creator. Obviously the possession of a tangible body would place some spatial limitations upon God. Accordingly, the question of whether or not God can be in more than one place at the same time has received some attention in Mormon literature. Attempting to preserve divine omnipresence, James E. Talmage, the church's foremost conservative theologian of the early twentieth century, developed an argument anticipated by his predecessors and employed frequently by his successors, asserting that God's influence can be felt throughout the whole universe. However, God is spatially limited—a position which Talmage argued on the basis of biblical anthropomorphism, such as God's moving from one place to another (1955, 42–43). In the Book of Abraham creation scripture, cited above, the gods "go down for there is space there" to "organize" matter into the universe. Space is conceived as if it were primal matter through which other matter can pass or travel, while, at the same time, it is also conceived of as a location or place. Even before the universe was created, its future location was identified in terms of the "space" which "is there," where it could be organized. Yet this space is real. It is irreducible matter that can neither be created nor destroyed.

The concept of a changing God, a God in the process of "becoming" rather than "being," permeates traditional Mormon theology and further illustrates God's temporality. God is not the creator of time, as Christian orthodoxy assumes, but exists within time. According to Mormon doctrine, God was not always God; he has changed and progressed. Again, in the King Follett Discourse, perhaps the most important of Joseph Smith's speeches, the Mormon prophet taught that "God himself was once as we are now, and is an exalted man, and sits enthroned in yonder heavens! That is the great secret." Smith continued:

> It is the first principle of the Gospel to know for a certainty the Character of God, and to know that we may converse with him as one man converses with another, and that he was once a man like us; yea, that God himself, the Father of us all, dwelt on an earth, the same as Jesus Christ himself did; and I will show it from the Bible (1938, 345–46).

In spite of the virtual canonization of Joseph Smith's position in the couplet "As man now is, God once was; as God now is, man may become," Mormonism has sometimes expressed confusion regarding the progressive nature of God. I suspect that the problem originates in other early Mormon teachings assuming a position similar to orthodox Christianity and the theological naivete of the church's "lay" clergy. For example, the third lecture of the 1835 "Lectures on Faith," which Joseph Smith certainly endorsed, if not authored personally, contains the following:

> But it is equally necessary that men should have the idea that he is a God who changes not, in order to have faith him . . . ; for without the idea of unchangeableness in the character of the Deity, doubt would take the place of faith. But with the idea that he changes not, faith lays hold upon the excellencies in his character with

unshaken confidence, believing he is the same yesterday, today, and forever, and that his course is one eternal round (J. Smith n.d., 36).

Instead of settling upon the idea of either an unchangeable or a progressing God, many Mormons have come to embrace both. Arguments exhibiting little appreciation for the implications of either concept are occasionally used to qualify unchangeability or to modify progression—usually both—in such a manner as to negate the advantages of either. However, most Mormon theologians have emphasized the changeability of God since even Mormonism's most exacting absolutists are unable to abandon the idea of divine progression (see J. F. Smith 1954; McConkie 1958).

At least from the time of the King Follett Discourse, Mormon theology found God to be the very embodiment of "eternal progression." Criticizing Orson Pratt, one of nineteenth-century Mormonism's more sophisticated absolutist theologians, Brigham Young declared:

> Some men seem as if they could learn so much and no more. They appear to be bounded by their capacity for acquiring knowledge, as Brother Orson Pratt, has in theory, bounded the capacity of God. According to his theory, God can progress no further in knowledge and power; but the God that I serve is progressing eternally, and so are his children: they will increase to all eternity if they are faithful (JD 11:286; see also Bergera 1980).

Ten years earlier, in 1857, Wilford Woodruff, one of Brigham Young's successors to the Mormon presidency, said:

> If there was a point where man in his progression could not proceed any farther, the very idea would throw a gloom over every intelligent and reflecting mind. God himself is increasing and progressing in knowledge, power, and dominion, and will do so worlds without end; it is just so with us (JD 6:120).

The idea of divine progression became a tenet of Mormon theology (see Bergera 1982). Even absolutists, who claim that God is the same yesterday, today, and forever, accept a unique Mormon concept of eternity that implies divine progression. In contrast with the classical Christian concept of eternity as a condition of timelessness—something beyond time—which necessarily follows from the *ex nihilo* creation, where God creates time along with everything else, most Mormons conceive of eternity as unending time, "everlastingness," "foreverness." Time—like God, matter, and space—exists necessarily. It is an environmental fact that God cannot alter. He, like everything else that exists, exists within and not beyond time. Moreover, this concept underscores the continuity between the sacred and secular—the *now* and the *then*—of Mormon thought in contrast with the radical discontinuity of orthodox Christianity.

This temporal character of God not only establishes his finitude but, in the context of Mormonism, presupposes natural and moral laws as universals. The path to godhood lies in the acquisition of the knowledge to understand these laws, the development of the skills to apply them, and the molding of the requisite character through obedience to

[margin handwritten notes, right side:]
McConkie 1958 p 318 makes this a proof text against the view that God was a God of wrath in the O.T., one of love in the N.T., as "liberal" religionists maintain.

So God commands it because it is moral — it is not moral only because God commands it.

eternal moral precepts. Thus Orson F. Whitney, a late nineteenth-century Mormon theologian, claimed that it is God's "superior intelligence that makes Him God," that the gospel is merely a ladder "of light, of intelligence, of principle" by which men become gods (*Deseret Weekly*, 25 May 1889). And B. H. Roberts, in a discussion of moral laws, wrote: "Good and evil then, in Latter-day Saint philosophy, are not created things. Both are eternal, just as duration is, and space. They are old as law—old as truth, old as this eternal universe. Intelligences must adjust themselves to these eternal existences; this, the measure of their duty" (1930, 2:404).

The idea of God as "becoming" rather than "being," God's spatial limitations, and the general environment in which moral laws, natural laws, and matter all exist necessarily combine to provide the finitism that characterizes traditional Mormon theology. Clearly, the omnipotence and omniscience associated with classical Christianity cannot justifiably be attributed to the Mormon God. This should not be construed, however, to mean that such absolutist language is absent from Mormon discourse. Like most Christians, many Mormons seem unable to resist the use of the "omnis" in their descriptions of deity. Even those Mormon writers who describe God as all-knowing and all-powerful typically embrace the metaphysics described above. Indeed, the problem for Mormonism arises not so often out of disagreement over the metaphysical basis of Mormon theology as out of a misunderstanding of the implications of this metaphysics for one's concept of God and the language of absolutism. A "typical" Mormon might conclude that God is omnipotent and omniscient while accepting Mormon metaphysics. He or she might not understand that Mormon metaphysics precludes an infinite God and necessarily implies that God must be finite since he exists within an environment over which he lacks complete control.

Lowell Bennion, a contemporary Mormon theologian, advocates a position that is consistent with Mormon metaphysics, by describing God as "most-powerful" rather than all-powerful. Asserting that God has tremendous power but not all power, Bennion assumes that even God cannot do everything he wills (1962). For instance, there are presumably occasions when God would like to reduce or eliminate the suffering of humans and other animals but lacks the power to do so. Under these circumstances, God can merely suffer with us. Bennion's position follows from an acute sensitivity to the problem of evil and an understanding of Mormon metaphysics. If his view is not widely held within Mormon circles, it is nonetheless compatible with a metaphysics that enjoys consensus. The concepts of omnipotence and omniscience appear in Mormon discourse as frequently as they do simply because Mormons, officials and laity, do not fully appreciate their meanings. Both are inconsistent with traditional Mormonism's doctrine of a finite God.

HUMAN NATURE

If traditional Mormonism's concept of God deviates from classical Christianity, its assessment of human nature is an even more radical departure. Denying the *ex nihilo* creation not only has implications for the absoluteness of God but, for Mormons, results in an affirmation of the necessary existence of humanity. Just as God exists necessarily, so do matter, space, time, natural and moral law, and "intelligence," the uncreated essence of human beings. Mormonism thereby denies the ultimate contingency of humankind.

That Joseph Smith recognized the radical nature of this doctrine and its implications for the orthodox Christian concept of human nature seems apparent. In 1833, he recorded a revelation which proclaimed that "Man was also in the beginning with God. Intelligence, or the light of truth, was not created or made, neither indeed can be" (D&C 93:29). And subsequently, in the King Follett Discourse, he reiterated this, explaining that his remarks were "calculated to exalt man." He chose to discuss "the soul—the mind of man—the immortal spirit. Where did it come from? All learned men and doctors of divinity say that God created it in the beginning; but it is not so: *the very idea lessens man in my estimation. I do not believe the doctrine; I know better*" (1938, 352; emphasis added). He continued,

> I am dwelling upon the immortality of the spirit of man. Is it logical to say that the intelligence of spirits is immortal, and yet that it had a beginning? The intelligence of spirits had no beginning, neither will it have an end.

There never was a time when there were not spirits; for they are co-equal [co-eternal] with our Father in heaven (ibid., 353).

If some confusion exists over the exact meaning of "intelligence" in Mormon theology, it typically has been conceptualized as something analogous to the ego, self, or, in the language of Joseph Smith, "the soul—the mind of man—the immortal spirit."[1] In one of the more perceptive essays on Mormon theology by an ecclesiastical authority, B. H. Roberts wrote, "There is that in man, according to our doctrine, [that] which is not created at all; there is in him an 'ego'—a 'spirit' uncreated, never made, a self-existent entity, eternal as God himself; and of the same substance or essence with him, and, indeed, part of him, when God is conceived of in the generic sense" (1903, 164). It is this assertion, that human intelligence is uncreated, that it shares with divinity its necessary being, that denies the ultimate contingency of humankind and provides the fundamental basis for an optimistic concept of human nature.

But traditional Mormon optimism is not limited to the denial of human contingency. It is boldly expressed in the claim that human nature is basically good, that an individual is "a God in embryo" (JD 23:65). Nor is the denial

---

[1] Smith is apparently not referring to the Mormon usage of these terms, for they have special meaning in Mormon theological discourse. Rather, he is referring to the general usage within the Christian tradition designating the essence of humanity. For an introduction to the Mormon concept of the pre-existence, see Ostler 1982.

of human contingency the only significant departure from Christian orthodoxy on the doctrine of human nature. On the contrary, the assertion of human goodness denies the human predicament proclaimed by classical Christianity. It assumes that the human predicament is not really a predicament at all, but that human beings are more good than evil. This, indeed, is a radical departure from orthodox Christianity.

In contrast to Catholic and Protestant orthodoxy, traditional Mormonism denies the doctrine of original sin. While Catholic theologians generally assert that humankind is in a state of sin because divine grace was withheld as a result of the Fall, Protestant theologians typically maintain that humankind is in a universal state of sin because of the corruption of human nature. It is important to note, however, that in both Catholicism and Protestantism all men and women are in a state of sin and can be saved only through the grace of God. Indeed, this is the meaning of the human predicament. Yet to be a sinner means more than to actually sin since sin is defined as a state or condition. To the most pessimistic theologians, human beings, as a result of their sinful condition, can do no good; they can only sin. They are lost and completely helpless. This doctrine of original sin, in which all humanity shares the guilt and estrangement from God, defines the human predicament in traditional Christian thought.

Nowhere is Mormon optimism regarding human nature more evident than in its denial of original sin that appears in several tenets of Mormon theology. First, Mormonism radically reinterpreted the Fall. In contrast to the Protestant notion that the Fall resulted in a condition of human depravity and the Catholic view that it led to a withdrawal of supernatural grace, the traditional Mormon position asserts that the Fall was a necessary condition for humanity to realize its ultimate potential. Humankind's premortal existence as intelligences and then spirits did not provide them with physical bodies which, in Mormon belief, are necessary to "experience a fullness of joy." Hence, an important consequence of the Fall was the acquisition of physical bodies. Beyond that, it was necessary to leave the immediate presence of God—to "enter the school of mortal experiences"—in order to overcome evil and develop the requisite moral character to realize the destiny of godhood (Talmage 1955, 69).

The real meaning of the Fall, then, is that it provided humanity with opportunities to obtain physical bodies and to gain experience. The Fall was part of God's plan for the benefit of his children. In a Mormon revelation, Adam and Eve praise God after being banished from the Garden of Eden.

> Blessed be the name of God, for because of my transgression my eyes are opened, and in this life I shall have joy, and again in the flesh I shall see God.
> And, Eve, his wife, heard all these things and was glad, saying: Were it not for our transgression we never should have had seed, and never should have known good and evil, and the joy of our redemption, and the eternal

life which God giveth unto all the obedient (Moses 5:10–11, in PGP).

This passage anticipates the Mormon propensity to regard the behavior of Adam as a "transgression" rather than a sin. Mormons usually avoid using "sin" to describe Adam's act of disobedience, for that act constituted a necessary condition for human mortality which itself is essential to human fulfillment. Mormon church apostle and theologian Orson F. Whitney, in a footnote to his lengthy poem, *Elias: An Epic of the Ages*, diminished the "sin" of Adam.

> There are two general classes of crimes—*malum per se* and *malum prohibitum*. *Malum per se* is a Latin phrase signifying "an evil in itself," while *malum prohibitum* means "that which is wrong because forbidden by law." The transgression of our First Parents was *malum prohibitum*, and the consequent descent from an immortal to a mortal condition was the Fall (1914, 128n7).

In other words, the Fall was an essential step in the eternal quest of humankind. A little more than twenty years ago, Sterling W. Sill, a Mormon official, wrote, "Adam fell, but he fell in the right direction" (*Deseret News Church Section*, 31 July 1965). And an often quoted passage of the Book of Mormon holds that "Adam fell that men might be; and men are, that they might have joy" (2 Ne. 2:25).

A second, though perhaps not as important, evidence of the Mormon rejection of original sin may be found in the status typically accorded Adam within Mormon theology. Instead of conceiving of Adam as the cause of human depravity and suffering, Mormonism holds Adam in high esteem. James Talmage deplored the "common practice" of heaping reproaches upon "our first parents" and declared that they "are entitled to our deepest gratitude for their legacy to posterity—the means of winning title to glory, exaltation, and eternal life" (1955, 70). Within Mormon theology, Adam is Michael the Archangel, the Ancient of Days. He assisted in the creation of the world, if not the universe, and will participate in resurrecting the dead at the Second Coming. He holds positions of importance next to the Godhead. Indeed, Adam was so highly regarded in nineteenth-century Mormonism that Brigham Young and other church leaders identified him as both the father of Jesus Christ and of humanity (see JD 1:50–52; Turner 1953; and especially Buerger 1982).

The concept of sin constitutes the third example of Mormonism's denial of the classical Christian doctrine of original sin. Sin, in Mormonism, is not a state or condition. Nor is it the human predicament. Sin is a specific act. Where Christian orthodoxy conceives of adultery as a consequence of human sinfulness, traditional Mormonism regards adultery, in itself, as sin. It is an act of disobedience to a commandment of God. It is, to be more precise, an act of breaking an eternal law.

This concept of sin can be illustrated by examining the meaning of repentance in Mormonism. Repentance is a turning away from sins, a refusing to commit them again. I use the plural rather than the singular to underscore the fact that repentance is the turning away from specific sins because for Mormons there are no others. Repentance is only possible because people can change. It is the process whereby the "sinner" stops sinning. Wilford Woodruff, a Mormon president during the late nineteenth century, declared that "the man who repents, if he be a swearer, swears no more; or a thief, steals no more; he turns away from all his former sins and commits them no more" (JD 23:127).

If Mormon discourse sometimes refers to humanity as "sinners," this should not be construed to mean a state of sin. It merely implies that all people, at some time, disobey eternal laws. However, people are not sinners for the same sins. Some are sinners because they lie, others because they steal. All can be said to be sinners only because none is yet perfect. No one has completely overcome all of his or her sins. Yet it should be recognized that Mormonism, like Protestant liberalism, maintains that humanity is perfectible. Indeed, the very goal of Mormonism is the perfecting of humankind. "Be ye therefore perfect, even as your Father which is in heaven is perfect," is a frequently quoted passage in Mormon sermons. This admonition of Jesus, to the Mormon mind, would be strange indeed were it impossible to fulfill. Parley P. Pratt, a theologically influential nineteenth-century apostle, argued that the notion that one cannot live without sin, that people cannot achieve perfection, was a false doctrine (in McMurrin 1965, 68). Perfection is a goal toward which the true Mormon must always strive.

Consistent with this concept of sin as an act, the assumption of human perfectibility, and the reinterpretation of the Fall, is the emphasis on freedom of the will found in Mormon theology. Not only does it constitute an explicit denial of the classical doctrine of original sin, it may also be the most radical concept of freedom of will found within the Christian tradition. At least the Mormon doctrine of free will suffers from few of the limitations found in Protestantism and Catholicism. While free agency, which is the Mormon term for freedom of the will, is sometimes spoken of as a "gift of God," this is fundamentally inaccurate because Mormon metaphysics imply that the will, or human agency, has its origin in the uncreated human intelligence—that, strictly speaking, it is independent of God. It too is an uncreated quality of human intelligence. This appears at least to be an implicit assumption underlying much Mormon discourse.

In a typical interpretation of Mormon scripture, John A. Widtsoe, a popular twentieth-century theologian and apostle, discussed a council at which the preexistent spirits of all future inhabitants of the earth rejected any imposition on the freedom of will of men and women; for such a condition, even if it assured universal salvation, would destroy the essential nature of humanity and its relationship to deity. Speaking of humankind's "earth-career," Widtsoe wrote:

> Though he might walk in forgetfulness of the past, and have dim visions of the future, he would be allowed a

free and untrammeled agency as he walked in the clear-
ness of the earth's day. While upon earth he might learn
much or little, might accept law or reject it, just as he
had been privileged to do in all the days that had gone
before (1952, 38–39).

The crucial point here is the unqualified claim that
humanity is free to do good or evil as a consequence of
their nature. There is no notion, as is frequently found in
Christian orthodoxy, that humankind can only choose to
act perversely. That is, men and women, because of the fall
of Adam, can only choose to sin. They are only partially
free. Such notions are foreign to Mormonism. While they
follow from conceptions of the Fall as the basis for original
sin, this concept of the Fall is, as I have argued, rejected by
traditional Mormons. The typical Mormon concept of the
Fall as the basis for implementing moral agency is entirely
consistent with this concept of complete freedom of will.
Moreover, it underlies a radical doctrine of salvation by
merit, which is also consistent with the traditional doctrine of deity.

A final argument for the denial of the doctrine of
original sin is indicated by Mormon proclamations that the
natural condition of humankind is good. Though occasionally one finds references to Paul's judgments of the "natural man" or to the Book of Mormon on the same theme
(see Mos. 3:19), Mormon literature typically avoids these
pessimistic depictions of the human predicament. In 1862,
Brigham Young told a congregation,

> It is fully proved in all the revelations that . . . [men and women] naturally love and admire righteousness, justice, and truth more than they do evil. It is, however, universally received by professors of religion as a Scriptural doctrine that man is naturally opposed to God. This is not so. Paul says in his Epistle to the Corinthians, "But the natural man receiveth not the things of God," but I say it is the unnatural man "that receiveth not the things of God . . . " The natural man is of God. We are the natural sons and daughters of our natural parents, and spiritually we are the natural children of The Father of Light and natural heirs to his kingdom; and when we do evil, we do it in opposition to the promptings of the Spirit of Truth that is within us. Man, the noblest work of God, was in his creation designed for endless duration, for which the love of all good was incorporated in his nature. It was never designed that he should naturally do and love evil (JD 9:305).

Young often argued that humanity is "naturally" good and attributed any inclination toward evil to "the force of example and wrong tradition." In a speech on "Man's Agency," he stated: "If a man had always been permitted to follow the instincts of his nature, had he always followed the great and holy principles of his organism, they would have led him to the path of life everlasting, which the whole human family are constantly trying to find" (1889, 82).

Despite some Calvinistic inroads into contemporary Mormonism (see the next chapter), most Mormon discourse retains the concept of the basic goodness of human nature. Hugh B. Brown, a member of the church's governing First Presidency from 1961 to 1970, expressed the more representative position in a 1964 General Conference speech:

> Our doctrine of man is positive and life affirming.
> We declare unequivocally that by his very nature every
> man has the freedom to do good as well as evil, that God
> has endowed him with a free moral will and given him
> the power to discern good from evil, right from wrong,
> and to choose the good and the right. We refuse to
> believe . . . that the biblical account of the fall of man
> records the corruption of human nature or to accept the
> doctrine of original sin. We do not believe that man is
> incapable of doing the will of God or is unable to merit
> the reward of Divine approval; that he is therefore totally
> estranged from God and that whatever salvation comes
> to him must come as a free and undeserved gift. We never
> tire of proclaiming the inspiring truth of the gospel that
> man is that he might have joy. For us the so-called fall of
> man placed the human spirit in a world of experience
> and adventure where evils are real but can be overcome,
> where free moral decision is a constant requirement, and
> where choices freely made, determine the quality of life
> and the eventual condition of the soul (CR, April 1964,
> 82).

In addition to the denial of the classical Christian
doctrines of original sin and the *ex nihilo* creation, traditional Mormon attitudes toward reason, science, and education attest to its optimistic assessment of human nature.
The common interpretation of several verses in Mormon
scriptures, not the least of which is the "glory of God is
intelligence" (D&C 93:36), exhorts Mormons to seek knowledge outside of religion. In fact, Mormonism defines areas
which are generally considered secular as the proper domain
of religion. It is necessary, as an obvious implication of Mormon metaphysics, to gain knowledge of the subject matter

of the physical sciences in order to understand the world, of the behavioral sciences in order to understand human nature, and of ethics in order to understand morality. As Thomas O'Dea, in an excellent sociological study of Mormonism, wrote: "The Mormon definition of life makes the earthly sojourn basically an educational process. Knowledge is necessary to mastery, and the way to deification is through mastery, for not only does education aid man in fulfilling present tasks, it advances him in his eternal progress" (1957, 147).

If a growing anti-intellectual trend is apparent in the church today, Mormon theology still retains a rational world view that requires faith in basic education. Mormons often hear that their religion embraces all truth, and this confidence in education is usually bolstered by quotes from Mormon leaders such as the following from Brigham Young:

> I am happy to see our children engaged in the study and practice of music. Let them be educated in every useful branch of learning, for we, as a people, have in the future to excel the nations of the earth in religion, science, and philosophy. Great advancement has been made in knowledge by the learned of this world, still there is much to learn. The hidden powers of nature which give life, growth, and existence to all things have not yet been approached by the wisdom of the world (JD 12:122).

Traditional Mormon optimism is equally apparent in its doctrine of salvation. Indeed, the goodness of humankind, the finitude of God, and humanity's potential for salvation by avoiding sin are concepts that combine to make

Mormonism an anthropocentric theology in contrast to the theocentric theology of classical Christianity.

SALVATION

Nowhere is the anthropocentric character of traditional Mormon theology more clearly evident than in the concept of salvation. Mormon doctrine differs significantly from the doctrines of grace that permeate orthodox Christianity. A Protestant scholar has called the "good news" that an infinite God wants to save depraved humanity from its predicament the essence of the Christian gospel (R. M. Brown 1966, 113). Such news, for the traditional Protestant, is especially good because humanity can do nothing to save itself. Indeed, we are lost. We cannot even participate in the salvation process. In the words of Emil Brunner, "even a partial clearing up of the contradiction on man's part" is impossible (1929, 56). The fundamental message of both orthodox and neo-orthodox Christianity is that humankind cannot save itself.

In contrast, Mormonism espouses a doctrine of salvation by works, evident in the emphasis on the Epistle of James. While Protestant and Catholic clergy quote Paul's "by grace are ye saved" and "not of works lest any man should boast," Mormon authorities typically quote James's "faith without works is dead." There is a virtual dearth of Pauline theology within traditional Mormon thought. Although Paul is quoted, it is on death, the resurrection, or his ethical exhortations. When Mormons do quote Paul on salvation, they typically misrepresent his concept of grace to mean that humanity will be physically resurrected by the gracious act of God. Traditional Mormonism denies classical doctrines of grace.

This does not mean that Mormonism has no concept of grace, but that Mormon concepts of grace differ from those of traditional and neo-orthodox Christianity. Like orthodox Christianity, Mormonism holds that mortality is a consequence of the Fall which is overcome through the atonement of Christ. Moreover, Mormon theology claims that as a result of the Fall humankind experienced a "spiritual death," a separation from the presence of God. Unlike Christian orthodoxy, this spiritual death did not alter human nature. It is not a condition of alienation in which the human/divine relationship has undergone some dramatic transformation, leaving the two in opposition to each other. On the contrary, the work and destinies of humankind and God remain interlocked. The meaning of "spiritual death" is to be cut off from the presence of God, not to be cut off from God. More importantly, this separation from the immediate presence of God is conceived of as a necessary condition for the development of humanity. It is through one's own meritorious efforts, along with the atonement of Christ, that he or she may be saved, transcend death, and return to the presence of God. Thus, it is essential to an understanding of Mormonism to recognize that the fall of Adam is a manifestation of the grace of God in as real a sense as the atonement of Christ. Both are necessary conditions for human fulfillment and the ultimate salvation of humankind.

I use the adjective "ultimate" to emphasize the difference between Mormon and traditional Christian concepts of salvation. Mormonism is not concerned with salvation, as it is typically conceived, but with exaltation. Nineteenth-century Mormonism, following the Universalists, embraced a doctrine of universal salvation, which profoundly affected subsequent doctrinal and theological elaboration. While Mormon notions of salvation typically refer to the universal physical resurrection of all humanity (D&C 76) or to the near universal extension of a "degree of glory" in heaven to all except those who sin against the Holy Ghost (ibid.), exaltation denotes returning to the presence of God and the realization of the ultimate potential of godhood. The exaltation of humankind is both the ultimate goal of Mormonism and the very work of God himself (Moses 1:36, in PGP). This is what Joseph Smith had in mind when he proclaimed:

> Here then is eternal life—to know the only wise and true God; and you have got to learn how to be Gods yourselves, and to be kings and priests to God, the same as all the Gods have done before you, namely by going from one small degree to another, and from a small capacity to a great one; from grace to grace, from exaltation to exaltation (1938, 346–47).

This concept of exaltation, which combines grace, sacramental, and merit doctrines of salvation, clearly reveals the eclecticism of traditional Mormon theology. Grace, as noted, is evident in the fall of Adam and in the atonement of Christ; both are necessary, though not sufficient, conditions for exaltation, which also requires submission to such sacraments as baptism, receiving the Holy Ghost, priesthood ordinations, and temple endowments. Yet, even when combined with the Fall and Atonement, these sacraments are insufficient. In popular Mormon parlance, people must also "work out their own salvation."

Accordingly, a doctrine of salvation by merit, consistent with Mormon metaphysics, obliges the devotee to acquire the requisite knowledge—secular as well as religious—to become like God. A Mormon revelation declares that "it is impossible for a man to be saved in ignorance" (D&C 131:6), and Joseph Smith spoke of the "principle of knowledge" as the "principle of salvation." Mormon theologian Orson F. Whitney stated:

> So says Joseph Smith. Intelligence is the glory of God. It is his superior intelligence that makes him God. The Gospel . . . is nothing more or less than a ladder of light, of intelligence, or principle, by which man, the child of god, may mount step by step to become eventually like his Father (*Deseret Weekly*, 25 May 1889).

If the "principle of knowledge is the principle of salvation," knowledge itself is insufficient. People must also live according to certain moral principles. They must live the commandments of God—the eternal laws. They must be more than hearers of the word. They must be doers, for it is only through obedience to the "laws and ordinances of the gospel" that they may be exalted. This emphasis on

works, or merit, is indicated by James Talmage's claim, cited
previously, that mortality is a "school" in which we learn
the differences between good and evil so as to help us overcome the latter. In *The Gospel and Man's Relationship to
Deity*, one of the better discussions of the basic principles
of the Mormon religion, B. H. Roberts described salvation
as a "character-building" process,[2] in which the disciple
must shun evil. Salvation comes by "resisting a temptation
today, overcoming a weakness tomorrow, forsaking evil asso-
ciations the next day, and thus day by day, month after
month, year after year, pruning, restraining and weeding
out that which is evil in the disposition, that the character
is purged of its imperfections" (1893, 264).

Yet, Roberts argued, overcoming evil does not fill
the requirement. People must also do good. They must "cul-
tivate noble sentiments by performing noble deeds," not
necessarily those deemed great by society but small, good
works. Roberts concludes his chapter on "Laws of Spiritual Development" by summarizing the meaning of exaltation.

> Thus by eschewing the evil inclination of the dispo-
> sition on the one hand, and cultivating noble sentiments
> on the other, a character may be formed that shall be
> godlike in its attributes and consequently its possessor

---

[2] Roberts does not use the term "character-building" in the edition
from which these quotes are taken. However, it is used in subsequent
editions and appears at least as early as in the fifth edition. The importance of Roberts's work was first pointed out to me by Sterling McMurrin (1965, 68-77).

will be fitted to dwell with God, and if so prepared, there is no question but his calling and election are sure (ibid., 265).

The traditional Mormon concept of salvation is fundamentally set apart from orthodox Christianity by its insistence upon the perfectibility of the individual and the imperative that he or she become like God. Because of this emphasis on merit, that people "work out their own salvation," the traditional Mormon doctrine of salvation, or exaltation, like the doctrines of God and human nature, stands as a heresy within the orthodox Christian tradition.

CONCLUSION

Whereas the God of Christian orthodoxy is absolute, the God of traditional Mormonism is necessarily finite. For the latter exists within an environment over which he lacks ultimate control. Matter, space, time, natural and moral law, uncreated intelligences, and God himself all exist together necessarily. Consequently Mormonism denies the *ex nihilo* creation which guarantees the hiatus between creator and creature in traditional and neo-orthodox Christianity. Moreover, the Mormon God changes. He progressed to become what he is today, and he continues to progress. He is more accurately characterized in terms of "becoming" than "being." God is not, in the vocabulary of classical Christianity, omnipotent, omniscient, or omnipresent, and references to him as such are, I believe, clearly inconsistent with traditional Mormon metaphysics.

The traditional Mormon concept of human nature, as I have argued, is an even more radical departure from Christian orthodoxy. Not only do humans exist necessarily, which is the ultimate basis for their freedom and autonomy, but the human situation is defined as good rather than evil. This is apparent in Mormonism's denial of the classical doctrines of original sin, reflected in its reinterpretation of the Fall as a necessary condition for human exaltation; in the high status accorded Adam; the defining of sin as an act rather than a condition; in the radical freedom of will attributed to humankind; and in the assumption that human nature is good rather than evil. The emphasis on reason, science, and education permeating much of Mormon culture further enhances its optimistic concept of human nature.

Following from these doctrines of God and human nature is a doctrine of salvation stressing merit rather than grace. If grace appears in both the Fall and the Atonement as necessary conditions for the salvation of humanity, then exaltation, which is the ultimate purpose of Mormonism and is the destiny of humankind, is thoroughly dependent upon works. It requires the observance of key sacraments, the acquisition of the requisite knowledge, and the development of the appropriate moral character.

It is, in fact, the traditional Mormon concept of exaltation, or the realization of godhood, that best expresses its peculiar American character. The idea of unlimited progress, which permeated American consciousness, became the "doctrine of eternal progression" among Mormons. The fluidity of the American class structure was projected onto the beyond with a religious imperative for social mobility. If God had attained his exalted status, human destiny was no less promising. Nowhere would the basic American values of work, achievement, mobility, and progress become more explicitly sacralized as cardinal tenets of a Christian theology. Thus, Mormon theology, like American cultural mythology, is preoccupied with "becoming" rather than "being." This unique doctrine of salvation, along with traditional Mormon concepts of deity and humanity, clearly differentiates its anthropocentricism from the theocentricism of Christian orthodoxy.

MORMON NEO-ORTHODOXY.

CHAPTER 4.

By emphasizing the differences rather than the similarities between God and humanity, Mormon neo-orthodoxy aligns itself more closely with Protestant neo-orthodoxy than with traditional Mormon thought. For instance, traditional Mormon theology teaches that humans were created in the physical and spiritual image of God and may themselves become gods. In contrast, Hyrum Andrus, an early neo-orthodox theologian and professor of religion at Mormon-owned Brigham Young University, lamented in a 1960 address at the school the Mormon preoccupation with anthropomorphic descriptions of God. Arguing that Mormons pay too little attention to the greatness of God, Andrus urged listeners to acknowledge divine uniqueness, or God's otherness. In fact, an emphasis on the "glory of God" generally characterized much of Andrus's writings.

Both traditional and neo-orthodox Protestantism emphasize the Creation in order to accentuate the differences between God and humanity. As products of the *ex nihilo* creation, humans owe their entire existence to God who is the source of all being. In traditional Mormonism, however, God does not bring nonexistent things into being but changes existing entities into forms better suited to their eternal progression. In other words, God's creative act changes humans from a primal form of intelligence into beings capable of becoming gods themselves. Among a majority of Mormons, the creation story is told not to emphasize the differences between God and humanity—to reveal the profound "otherness of God"—but to demonstrate God's love and concern for humanity whose inherent nature is to become co-creators with him.

Though Mormon neo-orthodox theologians typically accept the traditional metaphysics upon which these teachings rest, their telling of the creation story usually emphasizes the contingency rather than the necessity of humanity. David Yarn, a philosopher at Brigham Young University and one of the more articulate early representatives of this new Mormon theology, wrote:

> Mortals should take no special pride in the necessity of their original being, for they share this characteristic in common with all other things which exist. Furthermore, they would have remained in that original state were it not for God's goodness in having provided spirit bodies, the light of eternal truth, and opportunities for progression (1965, 152).

Thus according to Yarn, the necessary existence of "other things," such as space, time, and matter, implies that no meaningful consequence can be derived from the necessary existence of humanity.

Many Mormon neo-orthodox theologians further emphasize the otherness of God by reformulating the idea of a progressing God which Joseph Smith advanced in his later life. Like Smith, neo-orthodox Mormons believe that God was once a man who has progressed to his present status. Unlike Smith, however, they apparently believe that God is best described in terms of a synthesis of "becoming" and "being." With possible exceptions,[1] they are inclined to believe that God does not now progress in knowledge, power, or goodness. In these attributes, he is presumably absolute. Whatever "progression" he experiences is manifest only in increase over his dominions through the organization of new worlds. If he began finite, God has now become infinite. Having arrived at a point from which he can no longer progress, God possesses many, but not all, of the attributes of the classical Christian God.

When making such arguments, Mormon neo-orthodox theologians often cite the 1835 Lectures on Faith, originally printed as an introduction to one of the church's scriptures, the Doctrine and Covenants. Popularly attributed to Joseph Smith,[2] these lectures described God in the

---

[1]Andrus, for instance, in his Doctrinal Commentary on the Pearl of Great Price, attempted to reconcile the idea of a progressing God with Christian absolutism. Suggesting that God knows everything and has all power within his domain, he maintained that there are realms above God that God will attain through advances in knowledge and power (1967, 507).

[2]The authorship of the Lectures on Faith remains in question, with many scholars attributing most, if not all, of them, not to Joseph Smith, but to close associates Oliver Cowdery, Sidney Rigdon, and Frederick G. Williams (see Arrington 1969, 4; Gentry 1978). For my purposes, it makes little difference who wrote them. If Joseph Smith did, as most

vocabulary of classical Christianity. God is omnipotent, omniscient, and omnipresent. He is the same yesterday, today, and forever. He is unchanging and unchangeable. If he did not possess these attributes, he would not be an adequate object of worship for he would not be God (see J. Smith n.d., 36).

After quoting extensively from the *Lectures on Faith*, Yarn claimed in 1965 that Alma, a Book of Mormon prophet, correctly observed, "He [God] has all power, all wisdom, and all understanding; he comprehendeth all things, and he is a merciful Being even unto salvation, to those who will repent and believe in his name" (Al. 26:53). In *Know Your Religion*, Glenn L. Pearson, another Mormon neo-orthodox theologian of the early 1960's, and religion professor at Brigham Young University, claimed that humans are subject to law while God is not, for "God is infinite. Men are finite. God is not the servant of law but the master of it" (1961, 221). Lynn McKinlay, one of Pearson's colleagues at BYU, maintained, in a discussion of human agency, that God knows all things and has foreknowledge of all events (n.d., 33).

In spite of exposure to, if not formal training in, philosophy, theology, and related disciplines, most Mormon neo-orthodox theologians either ignore or dismiss con-

---

neo-orthodox theologians apparently assume, then he clearly reversed his position on the absolute nature of God in subsequent work. See J. Smith 1938.

flicts between traditional Mormon metaphysics and absolutism. This erosion usually assumes the depreciation of
reason in understanding God and the advocacy of a
nonreasonable, "alogical" form of revelation. Thus, Glenn
Pearson and Reid Bankhead wrote,

> There is hardly anything more clearly revealed in
> the scriptures than God's infinite foreknowledge; for every
> case of prophecy is witness of it. Yet many men do not
> believe it because their finite minds cannot grasp how it
> can be so if men are free to choose. If they cannot under-
> stand this, they at least ought to exercise enough faith to
> believe that if God says he has an infinite foreknowledge,
> it must be so. And if he says men are free, they must be
> free. And if he says both of these things, they must not
> conflict with each other (1962, 67).

Hugh Nibley, a professor of ancient scripture at
Brigham Young University and one of the more sophisticated neo-orthodox theologians, also dismissed the contradiction between Mormon metaphysics and absolutism. He
wrote, in response to intellectual demands that Mormonism conform to human reason, "A good example of this
[are the] . . . honest, persistent, and well-meant efforts to
convince our seminary and institute people that God simply *cannot* have foreknowledge of things, since that, according to an old and threadbare argument, would be incom-
patible with the free agency of man" (1960, 2).

Since the human mind is incapable of grasping these
and other mysteries, revelation for the neo-orthodox theologian becomes a way of both revealing the failure of human
reason and of affirming the otherness of God. The crucial

point here is that the revelation of human ineptitude is employed, much like the neo-orthodox use of the creation story and the concept of human contingency, to accentuate the differences between God and humanity. By emphasizing this human ineptitude as well as the contingency of humanity and the fact of creation, many Mormon neo-orthodox theologians establish the otherness and sovereignty of God.

However, neo-orthodox Mormons depart even more radically from traditional Mormon thought in their assessment of human nature. Where traditional Mormonism emphasizes human necessity, neo-orthodoxy underscores human contingency. That Joseph Smith recognized the radical nature of Mormon doctrine and the implications it posed for the classical Christian concept of human nature seems evident. In a speech defining the doctrine of the necessary existence of humans, Smith warned that his remarks were "calculated to exalt man," that the "very idea" of ultimate contingency "lessens man in my estimation" (1938, 353). Yet David Yarn argued that "mortals should take no special pride in the necessity of their original being. They, nevertheless, are contingent" (1965, 152).

Most Mormon neo-orthodox theologians minimize the implications of human necessity. Acknowledging that pre-mortal intelligence possessed free will in its uncreated state, Yarn explained that free will would have been lost in mortality were it not for Christ. When Adam fell, Satan "had for all intents and purposes destroyed the agency of man" (ibid., 33). This position is extended by other neo-orthodox theologians who have claimed that intelligence is merely "undifferentiated mass" from which God creates spirits. With this transformation of undifferentiated intelligence into spirits, "conscious entities" are "born." Not until humans reach this spirit state, which is a direct product of God's creative act, are they "egos," "selves," or "conscious entities." In contrast to traditional Mormonism, in which human essence is typically uncreated and coeternal with God, certain Mormon neo-orthodox theologians have argued that before God organized the human spirit, humanity was "undifferentiated mass" void of consciousness (see *Dialogue: A Journal of Mormon Thought* 2 [Spring 1967]: 5–6).

I believe that this emphasis on contingency is buttressed by an equally important departure from traditional Mormon thought—the neo-orthodox position on human nature. In contrast with the typical Protestant notion that the Fall resulted in a condition of human depravity and the Catholic concept that it led to the withdrawal of supernatural grace, the traditional Mormon view asserts that the Fall was a necessary condition for humans to realize their ultimate potential. The affirmation of the goodness of human nature follows from Mormonism's positive view of the Fall. Brigham Young challenged the Pauline notion that the natural man is an enemy to God:

> It is fully proved in all the revelation that God has ever given to mankind that they naturally love and admire righteousness, justice, and truth more than they do evil.

It is, however, universally received by professors of religion as scriptural doctrine that man is naturally opposed to God. This is not so. Paul says in his Epistle to the Corinthians, "but the natural man receiveth not the things of God," but I say it is the unnatural "man that receiveth not the things of God" (JD 9:305).

Although acknowledging the Fall as necessary for human exaltation, Mormon neo-orthodoxy typically emphasizes the negative consequences of the Fall. Rather than quoting those scriptural verses which describe the human condition in positive terms, the neo-orthodox emphasize such passages as the following from the Book of Mormon: "The natural man is an enemy to God and has been since the fall of Adam, and will be, forever and ever, unless he yields to the enticings of the Holy Spirit, and putteth off the natural man and becometh a saint through the atonement of Christ the Lord" (Mos. 3:19). They also adopt such traditional Christian terms as "carnal man," "sensual man," "devilish man," "original guilt," "evils of the flesh," and "seeds of corruption." Such language points to a pessimistic view of humanity. For example, while discussing Karl Marx, Pearson observed that "anyone who rejects Christ is already condemned since that which makes him reject Christ is the inherent wickedness already in him" (n.d.b, 2).

Similarly Yarn wrote that humanity is possessed of a "rebellious, perverse, recalcitrant, and proud disposition." But even as he described humanity as "carnal," "sensual," and "devilish," he cautioned readers not to confuse this with the "apostate doctrine of depravity." He was not suggesting that humans are born evil. The infant is born innocent, but, as he becomes accountable, through free decisions, he refuses to accept God and submit his will to him and thus is carnal, sensual, and devilish.

However, carnal, sensual, and devilish ought not to be interpreted in the most narrow sense. These words might be most accurately and broadly understood by the scriptural phrase "enemy to God." Not all "who have not made the covenants with the Christ are given to indulging in practices which are appropriately designated carnal, sensual, and devilish. Yet, all men, regardless of how moral and pure they may be with reference to those practices called carnal, sensual, and devilish, are enemies to God until they yield to the enticings of the Holy Spirit, accept the atonement of the Lord, and are submissive to his will" (1965, 129–30).

Since Mormon neo-orthodox theologians work within the context of Mormon metaphysics, their concept of the human predicament is not identical with Catholic or Protestant doctrines of original sin. They accept the traditional Mormon belief in the innocence of infants and perceive the Fall as having at least some positive consequences. Disclaimers to the contrary, Mormon neo-orthodoxy comes close to traditional Christian doctrines of human nature, though without abandoning important traditional Mormon beliefs. Hyrum Andrus, for example, defined sin in a way that is hardly distinguishable from Reformation doctrines of original sin. John Calvin, in *Institutes of the Christian Religion*, wrote:

> Original sin is a hereditary depravity and corruption of our nature, diffused through all parts of the soul, rendering us subject to the Divine wrath, and producing in us those works which the Scriptures call "works of the flesh." . . . [Thus,] the works which proceed from this condition, therefore, such as adultery, fornication, theft, hatred, murder, and orgies, [Paul] calls "fruits of sin," although they are also called "sins" in many passages of the Scriptures, and even by himself (1956, 25).

In his essay "Joseph Smith's Idea of the Gospel," Andrus advances a concept of original sin remarkably close to Calvin's position. Like Calvin, he observed that the seeds of corruption are "transmitted to each embryo at conception."

> The effects of Adam's transgression and of man's subsequent transgressions are transmitted in the flesh and are thus inherent therein at conception. It is said in a revelation that no less a personage than God explained this fact to Adam. After observing that the atonement took care of the legalities of the "original guilt," God said: "Inasmuch as thy children are conceived in sin, even so when they begin to grow up, sin conceiveth in their hearts, and they taste the bitter, that they may know to prize the good." Observe that it is when children begin to grow up that sin conceives in their hearts; and this because they are initially conceived in sin. Not that the act of conception, properly regulated, is sin, but the conditions of corruption resulting from the Fall are inherent in the embryo at conception. For a time the power of the atonement holds them in abeyance; but, as children grow up and begin to act upon their own initiative, sin conceives in their hearts. . . .

From this statement it is plain that men are not merely born into a world of sin. Instead, the effects of the Fall and the corruption that has subsequently become associated with the flesh are transmitted to each new embryo at conception. As the physical body develops, these elements of corruption manifest themselves by diverting the individual's drives and emotional expression toward vanity, greed, lust, etc. These elements of corruption are in the flesh (1961, 66).

The apparent distrust of human reason characterizing much of Mormon neo-orthodoxy serves to buttress this pessimistic concept of human nature. That sensory experience is unreliable is argued by neo-orthodox theologians who claim that the only way to acquire meaningful knowledge is through revelation (see, for example, Riddle n.d.; Nibley 1954). Consequently, they abandon interpretations of Mormon scripture traditionally used to encourage academic study. Andrus, for instance, reinterpreted the passage proclaiming that the "glory of God is intelligence"—used throughout Mormon history to encourage intellectual development—to mean that the "brilliant element" encircling God is "intelligence" (1965, 81–82); and Yarn reinterpreted the same passage to mean that intelligence refers to character rather than knowledge or learning (1965, 201–202). The scripture asserting that "it is impossible for a man to be saved in ignorance" was reinterpreted to mean that one cannot be saved without believing in Christ's divinity. Thus Yarn wrote,

> These words, as others previously discussed, have been used extensively to encourage people to seek excellence

in the traditional academic disciplines with the express intent that these were the things of which man could not be ignorant and be saved. And yet the context of this revelation, which is almost enthusiastically ignored, has little if any relation to the traditional academic disciplines, but does speak of one of the most sublime things available to mortals.

The knowledge of the truth, that is, Jesus Christ, the Redeemer of the world, and the principles which he has revealed. Not just the principles, but he in addition to the principles does and will make men free. The point is, even with the principles, and without him men could not ultimately be free (ibid., 203–204).

Such exegeses by Yarn, Andrus, and others, while characteristic of Mormon neo-orthodoxy throughout the 1960s and into the 1970s, are not representative of traditional Mormon thought. Together with the emphasis on human contingency, the denial of the basic goodness of human nature, and the formulation of a peculiarly Mormon doctrine of original sin, this depreciation of reason and reinterpretation of the role of education discloses Mormon neo-orthodoxy's repudiation of traditional Mormonism's optimism and reveals its affinity for a Protestant neo-orthodox conception of human nature.

The Mormon neo-orthodox doctrine of salvation also differs in tone, if not always radically in substance, from the traditional Mormon position. Neo-orthodoxy affirms fundamental Mormon belief in the afterlife but assumes a more restrictive path to salvation and greater reliance upon God. Indeed, it is this trend that tends to differentiate the neo-orthodox doctrine of salvation from that of traditional Mormonism. Nowhere is this more apparent than in the emphasis on grace, which necessitates a theocentric concept of salvation in contrast to the anthropocentric orientation of traditional Mormonism.

This is not to suggest that traditional Mormonism has no notion of grace. Both the fall of Adam and the atonement of Christ are examples of the grace of God. The Fall provided human beings with physical bodies and opportunities for obtaining knowledge and for developing moral character, while the Atonement provided for a physical resurrection and the opportunity for reunion with God. Like classical Christianity, traditional Mormonism assumes that human beings were separated from the presence of God as a consequence of the Fall; unlike classical Christianity, Mormonism declares that this "spiritual death" did not alter human nature or prevent mortals from being godlike.

Because of this optimistic assessment of human nature, traditional Mormonism does not emphasize the grace of God. In contrast with orthodox preachers who quote Paul's "by grace are ye saved," most Mormons rely more on James's "faith without works is dead." There is a significant absence of Pauline theology in traditional Mormonism, though Mormons often quote Paul. Mormons do quote Paul's moral exhortations, but typically reinterpret his concept of grace to mean that humanity will be physically resurrected through the gracious act of God.

The traditional Mormon doctrine of salvation is set

apart from classical Christianity by its emphasis on merit and insistence upon the perfectibility of the individual. Individuals must participate in various sacraments, such as baptism, receiving the Holy Spirit, and temple endowments, must obtain the necessary secular and religious knowledge, and must develop the requisite moral character to become like God. In contrast with classical Christianity, Mormonism emphasizes human rather than divine responsibility.

Retaining the sacramental element of traditional Mormonism's eclectic doctrine of salvation, neo-orthodox Mormons redefine the meaning of knowledge and the notion of moral development. Knowledge becomes more like traditional Protestant conceptions of belief, and character development is replaced with a doctrine of spiritual regeneration. These changes, which are consistent with neo-orthodox thinking on God and human nature, extend the Mormon neo-orthodox departure from traditional Mormon theology.

Neo-orthodoxy displaces the traditional Mormon imperative to seek knowledge, both secular and religious, to be saved. Thus, Yarn drew a dichotomy between "secular" and "redemptive" truth, with only the latter being necessary for salvation. He wrote,

> To call some truths secular does not mean they are valueless. It means they have a different value from those called redemptive. We know secular truths do have value for mortals. They may have value for post-mortals, and probably do, but to what extent they are needed we do

not know. Redemptive truths have value not only for mortals but are essential for post-mortals if they are to fulfill the true purpose of their being (ibid., 193).

Rejecting the notion that the gospel embraces all truth, Pearson argued that since the scriptures contain the gospel but not all known truth, "the gospel is not to be defined as all truth" (1961, 41–42):

> He who teaches that secular education and cultural attainment are part of the gospel, is either mixed up in his vocabulary or else on a foundation of sand. There are very excellent reasons for obtaining secular education and cultural attainment; but their acquisition does not constitute obedience to the gospel (ibid., 52).

This position implies a discontinuity between natural and supernatural realms that is generally foreign to traditional Mormonism. Many Mormon scholars have recognized the propensity of traditional Mormonism to reject a distinction between sacred and secular (see Arrington 1969; O'Dea 1957; McMurrin 1965). In traditional Mormonism, the continuity between the natural and supernatural is maintained by incorporating spheres usually regarded as secular into the sacred (such as the family, economics, and politics). By sacralizing the secular, traditional Mormonism tends to deny the secular; everything becomes religious. And all knowledge—natural, physical, moral, and spiritual—is essential to salvation. On the basis of these assumptions, the majority of Mormons claim that their religion embraces all truth.

The neo-orthodox break with traditional Mormon-

ism on the nature of character development is similarly significant. Consistent with its faith in the goodness of human
nature and its emphasis on the continuity of natural and
supernatural orders, traditional Mormonism emphasizes the
performance of good works. Defects in character are eradicated by behavioral changes. The individual stops being a
sinner by repenting and by not committing specific, actual
sins; there is, of course, no other kind of sin. Through such
actions, along with participation in the necessary sacraments
and the acquisition of the requisite knowledge, humans may
hope to realize Jesus' admonition that they become "perfect, even as your Father which is in heaven is perfect."

An apparent lack of concern for the gradual development of character through the performance of good works
characterizes Mormon neo-orthodoxy. Its doctrine of salvation requires a sudden, permanent, and total regeneration of human nature. Moral behavior is secondary to a
surrender of will through "spiritual rebirth." The central
task for the sinner is to put off the "natural man" and
become a saint through the atonement of Christ. The "transition from the realm of the natural to the spiritual," wrote
Andrus in the 1960s, "is required of all men, if they are to
obtain the good life here and salvation in the world to come"
(1965, 78). Failure to obtain and follow the Holy Spirit,
which is essential for this transition, condemns one to "do
the will of the flesh, by reason of the corruption which is
therein" (ibid.).

Mormon neo-orthodox theologians typically conceive of the turning away from specific sins not as an act of repentance but as a reform or moral change. Humanity needs a fundamental "regeneration," as Yarn wrote, to be "changed in the inner man" (1965, 74). Only through a "spiritual," not a "moral," change can humanity be saved. Pearson explained,

> One must repent "towards God." A reform is not enough if spiritual salvation is the goal. The intent must be to make oneself worthy of God's mercy and forgiveness. Repentance, in this sense, is a theological term, describing an act of compliance in the struggle to be saved, while reformation is an act inspired by an intelligent desire to improve one's lot in mortality (1961, 134).

Andrus also argued that human nature requires a thorough transformation. Liberals unfortunately try to "circumvent" this requirement "by stressing ethics and ideals without emphasizing that man must be regenerated by the powers of the Holy Spirit to achieve the Christian life" (1965, 90).

Certainly the neo-orthodox attempt to integrate Pauline theology with its classical Christian doctrine of grace into traditional Mormon metaphysics is understandable. But even exponents of this reconciliation have acknowledged that traditionally Mormonism has radically revised much of what Paul said. Pearson thus wrote,

> You know that we very often in the church nowdays think that Paul meant that the grace brought about the resurrection and that everybody would be resurrected by grace, but you notice that Paul said you are saved by grace through faith and you don't have to have faith to have

the resurrection and so we know Paul was speaking of another salvation other than the resurrection (n.d.a, 27–28).

This affinity with Paul has led most Mormon neo-orthodox theologians to emphasize the atonement of Christ in contrast to the life of Jesus that characterizes traditional Mormonism. Most Mormons point to the life of Jesus as the key to salvation and to perfection. Challenging (and thereby acknowledging) traditional Mormon practice, Pearson declared, it "is a grave offense to think that the mission of Jesus Christ was any other than the one involving his death" (1961, 108). Thus, to Mormon neo-orthodoxy, like Reformation and neo-orthodox Protestantism, the cross of Christ is more important ultimately than the life of Jesus.

THE CULTURAL CRISIS

During its first sixty years, Mormonism faced a series of profound social crises which threatened its very physical survival. Antagonists even succeeded in mobilizing resources of the United States government to eliminate the Mormon menace. Expectedly, this produced characteristic apocalyptic and martyrological theologies (described in chapter 2). In the twentieth century, such overt threats have been absent as Mormonism has successfully accommodated itself to American society. Rather, Mormonism has been challenged by cultural crisis, which undermines the cognitive foundations that endow social structures and behaviors with meaning.[3] This cultural crisis has helped to produce Mormon neo-orthodox theology.

Secularization, which was associated with the rise of Protestant neo-orthodoxy, refers to the loss of social influence for religious thought, behavior, and institutions. Secularization is largely a result of increasing functional rationality in economic and social life (e.g., bureaucracy) and the rationalization of thought (e.g., science) accompanying social differentiation. At the very least, secularization in twentieth-century America has helped to create an environment of religious pluralism where churches, like economic enterprises, must compete with one another (Berger 1967, 126–53).

No longer monopolies, most religious groups, by adapting to the pluralism of secular societies, have adopted bureaucratic structures, formulated goals reflecting a preoccupation with results, and conceptualized problems in terms of public relations. That Mormonism has adapted to secularization at the institutional level is evident in its elaboration of a hierarchical structure which relies on professional administrators to carry out routine operations, the

---

[3]Some non-Mormon scholars find the vitality of contemporary Mormonism results from its ability to adapt to its environment (see, for example, O'Dea 1957; Leone 1984). While much of the scholarship on twentieth-century Mormonism has concentrated on the church's successes, Mormon accommodation has not been without conflict. Sometimes the emphasis on success can lead to insufficient attention to the conflicts.

"rationalization of result-oriented administrative procedures," and the "dominance of bureaucratic logic in such areas as public relations, political lobbying, fund raising and financial investments in the secular economy" (Shepherd and Shepherd 1984b, 32).

In an insightful content analysis of Mormon semi-annual General Conference addresses from the beginning of the church to 1980, Gordon Shepherd and Gary Shepherd found compelling evidence of the impact of secularization on the sermons of Mormon officials. They tested hypotheses derived from Peter Berger's analysis—which assumes a greater flexibility of beliefs, a diminishing preoccupation with the supernatural, more concern for personal morality and family issues, and a tendency to embrace standard tenets of the general religious tradition—and found a pronounced trend in each of these predicted directions since 1920. Yet, they also reported that Mormonism retained considerable sectarianism with "a perceptibly renewed concern about the encroaching dangers emanating from the values, life styles, and political directions of the secular world" (Shepherd and Shepherd 1984a, 145–46). Thus, in spite of Mormonism's adaptation to secularization, the Shepherds rejected Mark Leone's assumption that the appeal of modern Mormonism derives from "doctrinal flexibility" (see Leone 1984; cf. White and White 1981; Shepherd and Shepherd 1984a, 10–12). The Shepherds concluded that

> perhaps the primary appeals of Mormonism in the modern world are not so different from what was offered by

the vision of the Mormon kingdom in the nineteenth century: authoritative centralized leadership, moral certitude, a strong sense of community identification and active involvement in a transcendent cause. Like other conservative religions in modern society, Mormonism functions largely as an alternative to the confusing diversity and moral ambiguity of modern secular life (1984b, 40).

If Mormonism has succeeded in adapting to secularization at the institutional level and shown remarkable accommodation regarding some beliefs, its efforts at resisting secular society in other respects remain a hallmark. The Mormon emphasis on personal morality and family issues reflects resistance to secular trends as much as accommodation. Accommodation is implied when a religious movement retreats to these areas as its sole or primary concern, but resistance is involved when stands on personal morality and family issues contradict secular trends. While many Protestant denominations accommodated the "sexual revolution" of the 1960s by further accepting divorce, sexual relations outside of marriage, and cohabitation, Mormons reaffirmed traditional sexual norms by embracing premarital chastity and repudiating birth control, recreational sex, and abortion (see Mauss 1976; W. Smith 1976; Christensen and Cannon 1978; Christensen 1982; Rytting and Rytting 1982). Mormons have also rejected secular concerns over the population explosion and trends toward smaller families, greater equality among the sexes, and the redefinition of gender roles (see Bush 1976; Heaton and

Calkins 1983; White 1984; White 1985; White and White 1982a).

Such resistance was anticipated in E. E. Ericksen's early social scientific study of Mormonism, *The Psychological and Ethical Aspects of Mormon Group Life* (1922). Dividing Mormon history into three stages of "maladjustment" involving confrontations with (1) non-Mormons, (2) nature, and (3) "new thought and old institutions," Ericksen saw the final stage as a conflict between Mormonism and secularization. This cultural crisis would intensify as the Mormon educational level increased and heretical ideas were introduced into religious circles. Ericksen predicted an increase in apologetics with the express purpose of "justifying the Mormon dogmas." He wrote:

> This peculiar rationalizing has developed side by side with heresy which it is constantly endeavoring to silence by argument. Besides a large number of books written with this aim, the church theological classes are making use of this line of reasoning. The old institutions and traditions are thus fortified on the one hand by sentiments and on the other hand by a well-developed system of theology.
>
> Opposed to these conservative Mormon theologians stand those who are effectively bringing about a readjustment in both thought and sentiment. These people do not present direct opposition. They tend to shift the attention to more vital problems of the day. They emphasize the present rather than the past, the immediate rather than the remote, the concrete rather than the abstract (ibid., 98).

Following this tradition, Catholic sociologist Thomas

O'Dea subsequently argued that "Mormonism's greatest and most significant problem is its encounter with modern secular thought" (1957, 244). In a special foreword to a new edition of Nels Anderson's *Desert Saints*, O'Dea observed:

> The urbanization of the Wasatch Front area of Ogden, Salt Lake City, and Provo, the development of modern business and the creation of modern tastes for consumer goods and an affluent life, the rigidification of church organization into older patterns not necessarily appropriate to new conditions, and the inevitable secularization of Mormon life are all in advanced stages of development. All the problems of modern society—from juvenile delinquency to the mounting toll of highway deaths—are now to be found in the kingdom of the Saints. Moreover, Utah has three universities which confront young Mormon minds with modern thought. Impersonalization of life, religious crisis and doubt, and a search for new values and new identities can also be found (Anderson 1966, xviii).

Certainly, the impact of modernity on Mormonism has intensified with education. According to O'Dea, education has produced within Mormonism a " 'transmission belt' that would bring into Zion all the doubts and uncertainties that, in another century, were to beset the gentile world" (1957, 225). In addition, increased contact with the outside world has produced further interest in new life styles, social relations, patterns of thought, and institutional forms. Specialization has encouraged secularization by limiting the function and influence of religion. In Utah, as well as the nation, greater power has accrued to government, education, and science, dislocating individuals and collectivities

with vested interests in the older, more sacred social patterns. Those so dislodged become, according to Daniel Bell,
the "generational dispossessed" who resist modernity (1963).
Through the 1950s and 1960s, many Mormon leaders and
emerging neo-orthodox theologians expressed a desire to
isolate their community from the growing influence of government, science, and education as well as the encroach-
ment of new life styles and social movements.[4]

The social movements and emergent life styles of the
1960s challenged fundamental American customs and
beliefs. Racial and minority group confrontations revealed
deep-seated racism; a false sense of prosperity became evident with the rediscovery of poverty; the unrelenting war
in Vietnam convinced many at home and abroad that America was immoral and imperialistic; the entrenched bureaucracy of political and educational institutions was evidence
to many young people that the United States was no longer
democratic; and the realization that modern technology—
the culmination of fundamental American values—had created an environment which endangered human survival
shocked many Americans. If some people tended to see a
new world emerging out of this social milieu, others saw
the disintegration of their culture.

That many Mormons would be among those who

---

[4]To be sure, neo-orthodoxy is not the only reaction to secularization in Mormonism. It is, however, a theologically sophisticated response
that deserves serious attention.

found these changes threatening is not surprising since Mormonism had, by the end of the 1930s, incorporated fundamental American social and political values in its theology and religious practice.[5] The Puritan work ethic, for instance, may have become secularized in the "spirit of capitalism," but for Mormons it had been resacralized in the doctrine of eternal progression (see White 1980). Perhaps even more significant, however, were the beliefs Americans and Mormons shared concerning the destiny of their country and its role in world affairs. Mormonism buttressed its nationalism with religious meaning and fervor through revelations and a post-millennial theology in which America becomes the Promised Land and where the Kingdom of God must be established in preparation for Jesus' second coming (see Hansen 1974; Heinerman and Shupe 1985; cf. Gottlieb and Wiley 1984). Thus, America was not merely the future capital of the world, but, in the meantime, the guardian of liberty, freedom, and justice.

This is the context in which Mormonism's political conservatism and marked anti-Communism, in addition

---

[5] O'Dea went so far as to suggest that Mormonism is America "in miniature" and "presents a distillation of what is peculiarly American in America." He argued that this relationship between Mormonism and America justifies the study of Mormonism as a means of better understanding American society itself. In other words, Mormonism is conceived as a microcosm of the society with many of the larger strengths and weaknesses more graphically manifest. See his foreword to Anderson 1966. See Arrington 1966 for a similar argument regarding Mormon economic experience.

to its neo-orthodoxy, may be best understood. Throughout the post-World War II Cold War era, Mormon president David O. McKay defined the conflict between Communism and Christianity as the major struggle (see McKay 1964). Mormons attended few General Conferences without listening to warnings of the dangers of "godless Communism" and "creeping socialism," while the efforts of apostle Ezra Taft Benson, and others, to identify the church with the John Birch Society invited increased public scrutiny (see Gottlieb and Wiley 1984, 75–79). Elder Benson, in particular, seldom missed an opportunity to warn of the Communist take-over of America—a process which had begun with the reforms of the New Deal (see Benson 1961).

If Mormon officials such as President McKay and his first counselor J. Reuben Clark, Jr., were less preoccupied with Communist infiltration, they nonetheless encouraged the activities of Apostle Benson and BYU president Ernest L. Wilkinson by identifying Communism as America's most serious challenge. Interpreting the statements of church leaders as a mandate for implementing his conservative political agenda at BYU, Wilkinson tried to suppress student dissent with threats of expulsion, denied public forums to speakers and topics he termed "liberal," and intimidated some members of his faculty through covert surveillance and partisan hiring, firing, and promotion practices (Bergera and Priddis 1985, 173–226).

Wilkinson's general reaction to modernity could

hardly be more explicit than the litany of evils he presented in a 1966 Brigham Young University commencement address:

> In our day
>   1) when the Supreme Court has severely restricted prayers in schools;
>   2) when secularism is rampant on our campuses;
>   3) when students (fortunately just a minority) openly proclaim their defiance of our government and give aid and comfort to the enemy by burning their draft cards and promoting strife and disorder in protest against American soliders in Viet Nam, who are there to liberate the Vietnamese people;
>   4) when presidents of universities sit supinely by and allow students, in complete disregard of property rights, to seize and control university buildings, thereby giving encouragement to flouting the law;
>   5) when educators and ministers are teaching that "God is dead" and that there is not authentic objection to "free love";
>   6) when teachers and nurses degrade their professions by employing the coercive tactics of a labor union;
>   7) when civil disorder and defiance of law is carried on and tolerated under the guise of "academic freedom" and civil rights;
>   8) when, in short, the people of our country, for the solution of their problems, have chosen to rely upon the mandate of government and minority violence, rather than upon God and the sweat and toil of their own brows, we at this University still believe in and adhere to the simple instruction of Brigham Young (1966, 3-4).

While the Vietnam War divided American society, it only strengthened the resolve of Mormon anti-Communists. "Drop these suicidal 'limited political objectives' and launch a massive military campaign,'' declared Elder Benson. ''Topple the Hanoi regime, and dictate rather than negotiate the peace terms'' (1969, 11; see also Rector 1969; Bergera and Priddis 1985, 183). Even in ostensibly nonpolitical speeches, Wilkinson could not resist the temptation to condemn ''creeping socialism'' and the New Deal (see 1967, 11). For Wilkinson, his mission as BYU president lay in the recruitment and preservation of a patriotic faculty who would teach ''correct economic doctrines'' to save the American free enterprise system from ''threatened extinction'' (see Bergera and Priddis 1985, 173–226).

During the 1960s, these and other politically conservative Mormons enjoyed the support of several neo-orthodox theologians, some of whom appear to have been just as vocal in their denunciation of modern society as in their explication of theology. While the anti-Communism of the John Birch society appealed to some Mormons, its excesses offended others. Consequently, Mormon neo-orthodox theologians Hyrum Andrus, Reid Bankhead, and Glenn Pearson—all of whom more or less embraced Birchist ideology—had to be reminded at BYU not to ''interject their personal opinions and feelings in the classroom'' (Bergera and Priddis 1985, 196). Pearson, in an unpublished paper on ''Socialism and the United Order or the Law of Consecration,'' denounced further democratization in the United States because

> the franchise may be used as a means to introduce measures which will slowly, but inexorably deprive the citi-

zens of their property and productive will. These measures consist of such things as the destruction of sound money (so that inflation may be used as a form of taxation), the establishment of a graduated income tax, government regulation of prices and production, free compulsory education, government owned postal service and other businesses, and various types of government insurance, etc. (n.d.b).

Elsewhere, Pearson, perhaps the most politically vocal of all neo-orthodox theologians, asserted that God never intended that the United States should have a "social security program" (n.d.a, 15), while his BYU colleague Daniel Ludlow perceived the modern "welfare state" as a concerted attempt at moral disintegration to ensure that America would not realize its post-millennial destiny. Ludlow suggested that if he were Satan he would "hamper, and if possible, I would destroy the judicial system of every country on earth, because that is the system that has been given the responsibility for upholding law and order. And particularly I would set my sights on America, and I would do everything I could to destroy this bastion of free agency and free enterprise" (1970, 6).

Most neo-orthodox theologians were not mere advocates of free enterprise but appeared to posit laissez-faire capitalism as the Christian social ideal. Arguing that private enterprise is inherently more efficient, Chauncey Riddle claimed that if government had to "compete with private enterprise on an equal basis and pay the consequences [out] of its own funds, it would go down the drain rather rapidly" (1965, 9). Pearson condemned public welfare programs as "legal plunder" (1967b) and even denounced democracy itself (1967c). His reaction to modernity was apparent in his lamenting the loss of religious control over education with the development of the public school system. Denying the fundamental tenets of Christianity, public schools promoted a "state religion" perpetuated by public school teachers as "state supported clergy." Undergirding this state religion "is the ethic of socialism and democracy." Evidently democracy is evil because it is inherently "wasteful," "graft-infested," "compulsory," encourages "public robbery," and is a "paradise for bureaucrats" whether falling under the guise of the "New Deal," the "Fair Deal," the "Great Society," "civil rights," or "state welfare." No "Christian who understands Christianity and democracy," he wrote, "can believe in democracy" (ibid.).

Few issues provided a more visible symbol of the confrontation that gave rise to the development of Mormon neo-orthodoxy than the denial before 1978 of the Mormon priesthood to blacks. O'Dea, who had argued in 1957 that the church's strength and success derived from its capacity to adapt to its environment, contended in 1972 that the race issue had come to symbolize the Mormon encounter with modernity. Revealing all the "strains and conflicts" that he had previously identified with the secularization of Mormonism—literal versus critical interpretations of scripture, unquestioning obedience versus democracy, and political conservatism versus social idealism—O'Dea claimed that this issue would be the ultimate test of Mormonism's ability to come to terms with modernity. This was the only instance in which O'Dea questioned the likelihood of Mormonism's adapting meaningfully to its environment.

Before the 1978 decision to admit black males to the priesthood, the issue had become the source of considerable conflict within the Mormon community (see White and White 1980; Mauss 1982; White and White 1982b; Mauss 1981; Bush and Mauss 1984). Prior to the emergence of the civil rights movement, internal conflict had become apparent when church leaders considered establishing a mission in Cuba in the 1940s. Concerned about racial purity, they sought the advice of Mormon sociologist Lowry Nelson, who had done extensive research in Cuba. In June 1947, Nelson replied: "It would be better for the Cubans if we did not enter their island—unless we are willing to revise our racial theory. To teach them the pernicious doctrine of segregation and inequalities among races where it does not exist, or to lend religious sanction to it where it has raised its ugly head would, it seems to me, be tragic. It seems to me that we just fought a war over such ideas" (Nelson 1985, 337; see also White 1972, 40–41). This exchange ended when the First Presidency shortly reiterated that the priesthood denial originated in revelation to Joseph Smith and a warning that they were not "too impressed with the reasonings of men, however well founded they may seem to be" (ibid.). In 1951, the First Presidency issued an official statement declaring that the church position remained as it always had, that the priesthood denial was a product of revelation and not a caprious policy of the church (ibid.).

That the decade of the 1950s was characterized by increased conflict within the church is evident from arguments defending segregation by some Mormon officials (see White 1972, 45–46) and specifically by Apostle Joseph Fielding Smith's admission that church leaders had received "a flood of correspondence from all parts of the Church asking how it is that" the church "teaches a doctrine of segregation" (J. F. Smith 1958, 184). While leaders became more and more defensive of the church's racial policy, the die had been cast in the Nelson correspondence: the ban was a direct result of revelation and only through revelation could it be rescinded. Consequently, any criticism of Mormon racial practice was interpreted as an attack on the authority of the church itself. To reject the church's position was to deny revelation, and this was tantamount to questioning the legitimacy of the institution.

Politically conservative Mormon leaders vigorously defended the priesthood ban and sometimes segregation. Apostle Benson, for example, charged that the Communists were "using the civil rights movement to promote revolution and eventual takeover of this country" (in Turner 1966, 255). And Ernest Wilkinson, upon learning that the president of Stanford University had severed relations with BYU, declared that "in his man-made wisdom, he rejects one of our revealed beliefs" (1970, 7).

Most, if not all, neo-orthodox theologians embraced

the official position on blacks, and some of them produced elaborate apologetics to defend it. For example, Daniel Ludlow argued that the protests were not sincerely motivated criticisms of Mormon racial practice, but were a concerted effort to destroy freedom of religion in America (1970, 9). In his defense, Chauncey Riddle insisted that the church could only change under direction from God and that "we will not trust ourselves, we will not trust simply our reason, we will try to serve the Lord" (n.d., 11). Hyrum Andrus presented an argument that combined two explanations. Claiming that blacks were descendents of Cain, who was "cursed with a black skin" and denied the priesthood, Andrus asserted that the priesthood ban was a result of something blacks had done in their premortal existence. Cain's lineage was preserved beyond the Flood by Ham, a son of Noah, who had married a black woman (Andrus 1967, 400–407).

Hugh Nibley entered the controversy. Responding to Lester Bush's 1973 seminal analysis of the ban, Nibley identified Bush's lengthy article as "indispensable" but "strangely irrelevant." Like previous apologists who emphasized the awesome responsibility associated with the priesthood, Nibley came to the conclusion that for blacks the priesthood denial was actually a blessing not a curse.

> Nothing sounds more brutal and direct than Brigham Young's, "The negro must serve!" But what is so bad about serving in the light of the Gospel? "The son of

Man came not to be served, but to serve," meek and
lowly, a man of sorrows and acquainted with grief,
despised and rejected . . . need we go on? His true fol-
lowers will take up the same cross, "In this world ye shall
have tribulation," for "if the world has hated me, it will
hate you." The greater the tribulation here the greater
the glory hereafter, while he who is exalted in this world
shall be abased in the next. If we really took the Lord's
teachings seriously, we would be envious of the Negroes
(1973, 76).[6]

Nibley also alluded to the Mormon belief that a child
who dies before reaching the age of accountability (usually
eight years) automatically inherits a "celestial glory." He
concluded that "very few present-day priesthood-holders"
would reach the Celestial Kingdom; however, those who
did would be among millions of blacks since "the vast majority of Negroes who have lived on the earth have died as
little children" (ibid.). Even the inordinately high infant
mortality rate that has plagued the black community
appeared to demonstrate the ironic benevolence of an inscru-
table God.

If this seems unreasonable, then Nibley has succeeded
with his basic point. Denial of the priesthood to blacks was
not rational and could not be evaluated in "worldly terms."

---

[6]Nibley's response is characteristic of Mormon apologists who found
the terrible responsibility of the priesthood to border on a curse when
they defended its denial to blacks, or when they continue to do so with
regards to women who, like black men before 1978, cannot hold the
Mormon priesthood. On other occasions, the blessings of the priesthood and the opportunities it provides to act in God's name are stressed,
as frequently occurs in Mormon priesthood manuals and meetings.

Like the gospel itself, the priesthood ban was one of those supreme ironies that are never what they appear to be. Paraphrasing C. S. Lewis, Nibley reminded Mormons:

> It is the very contrariness and even absurdity of the Christian teachings that provide, for him, the highest proof of their divinity—this is no man's doing. In the efforts of every President of the Church to explain our position to the world, as presented in Dr. Bush's study, we see the admission that this thing is not the invention of those men—they are embarrassed by it, and they all pass the acid test for honesty when they refuse to put their own opinions forth as revelation—which in their case would have been an easy thing to do (ibid., 74).

Presumably, according to Nibley's argument, the more absurd a belief or practice the greater its claim to truth. Nibley's apologetics functioned much as those of other neo-orthodox theologians—they reinforced the literal interpretation of scripture, encouraged unquestioning obedience and acceptance of authority, and helped to perpetuate the conservatism O'Dea had identified as indicative of Mormonism's growing incapacity to come to terms with modernity.

[handwritten marginal note: Tertullian: "I believe because it is absurd."]

The race issue, which reflected Mormonism's encounter with modernity, was intertwined with the church's experience with secular education. No issue would become more significant than secular education for contemporary Mormonism's cultural crisis.

The modern study of religion implicitly challenges the underlying premises of older, more sectarian approaches to religion. In the modern study of the Bible, for instance, the scholar approaches the text as he or she would any other literary work. The Bible receives no special immunity simply because it is the Bible. The modern biblical scholar seeks to put aside theological prejudices in an attempt to reconstruct a text as close to the original as possible or to answer the questions of who wrote the document, to whom was it addressed, why, when, and within what context.

While some scholars study religious beliefs to understand their origins, relationship to behavior, functions for individuals and society, or to assess their truth-claims, others examine religious institutions to ascertain their origins, functions, patterns of development, and relationships to other social, political, and economic institutions. The discoveries from disciplines not directly concerned with religion may be perceived as threatening to religious world views. This occurred in physics with the Copernican revolution and in biology with the Darwinian revolution and the development of evolutionary theory. Though neither had any actual bearing on the existence of God, or even the question of human nature, they became sources of controversy among many Christians.

Nor was Mormonism exempt. No sooner had the push toward accommodation occurred in the early twentieth century than the issues of biblical criticism and biological evolution appeared among the Saints. That a significant cultural crisis would emerge on the heels of the resolution of the Mormon social crisis is not surprising given the historical value of secular education to Mormons. The faith that traditional Mormonism expressed in education logically followed from its metaphysics, its conception of human nature, and its "this-worldliness" that required the saints to "gather" to Zion to "build" the Kingdom of God in preparation for Jesus' second coming. Not only would knowledge and education ameliorate social ills, they would vindicate Mormon claims to truth. Indeed, traditional Mormonism's propensity to deny the distinction between sacred and secular is a result of its sacralizing of the secular. This means, of course, that the pursuit of knowledge typically considered secular was a sacred obligation. This emphasis on secular education helps explain the remarkable educational achievements of the Latter-day Saints.[7]

By stressing the importance of secular education, Mormonism has transformed an external crisis into an internal crisis. On the one hand, the church encourages secular education, even defining it as essential to salvation; on the other, secular education often dilutes Mormon orthodoxy and challenges its institutional forms. In the first instance, secular education constitutes a commandment; in the sec-

---

[7]Judging from the frequency of the appearance of Utahns in *American Men of Science*, *Who's Who in America* and *Leaders in Education*, E. L. Thorndike concluded in 1943 that Utah produced more eminent persons per capita than any other state. More recently, Kenneth Hardy's 1974 analysis of the social origins of American scientists and scholars found a disproportionately high number from Mormon and Jewish backgrounds.

ond, it poses a threat. Yet, the church itself sets the stage for a fascinating drama: many young people who later leave the church go to college convinced that they are following a divine commandment only to discover that their newly acquired ideas may make them unwelcome in church. In a sense, the church finds itself in the awkward position of potentially sowing seeds of discontent by creating a "transmission belt," to use the language of O'Dea, "that would bring into Zion all the doubts and uncertainties that, in another century, were to beset the gentile world" (1957, 225).

This crisis has elicited varied responses from Mormon leaders. Some have retained considerable confidence in education, and they have either attempted or encouraged the reconciliation of science and religion. The Mormon presidency in 1921, for instance, apparently endorsed the intent and sincerity of biblical critics. Commenting on the Jonah story, they agreed with "higher critics" that "the purpose and intent of the book are excellent and have several very grand lessons. These constitute the balance of the work. It is of little significance whether Jonah was a real individual or one chosen by the writer of the book to write what is set forth therein" (in Bergera and Priddis 1985, 50).

Notwithstanding an embarrassing and controversial incident at Brigham Young University in 1911, in which one professor was fired and two resigned for teaching evolution and biblical criticism, a number of Mormon leaders have expressed sympathy, if not open support, for evolutionary theory. Apostle John A. Widtsoe's "scientific theology," which included implicit acceptance of organic evolution, emphasized an underlying harmony between revealed truths and scientific discoveries (see 1952; 1960). His works enjoyed considerable popularity; in fact, it is not uncommon today to hear Mormon scientists respond to queries with Widtsoe's answers. Moreover, Mormon scientists, often with impressive academic records, are typically held up to the youth as examples of men and women who have pursued secular education while retaining their commitment to Mormonism.

In contrast, the public response of most Mormon leaders to this cultural crisis has tended to be antiintellectual. These men are convinced that Mormon theology needs no rational elaboration or defense. To write a column such as Widtsoe's "Evidences and Reconciliations" was to admit that reformulation is necessary. Assuming a posture similar to the Protestant fundamentalists in their confrontation with modern science, the antiintellectualism of these Mormons discounts the need to come to terms with secular thought. Only that knowledge from science that conforms with their religious presuppositions is acceptable.

While the most vocal representatives of this antiintellectualism among ranking Mormon authorities during the past two decades have been Ezra T. Benson, Bruce R. McConkie, Mark E. Peterson, and Boyd K. Packer, the twentieth-century tendency toward anti-intellectualism received its basic articulation and legitimation from the late J. Reuben Clark, Jr. As a counselor in the First Presidency from 1933 to 1961, Clark employed his status to remove people from positions where they might encourage a more intellectual development of Mormon theology (see Quinn 1983, 172–95; Bergera and Priddis 1985, 60–65). Addressing faculty of the church's educational system, he said that Mormon youth are "not doubters but inquirers, seekers after truth. Doubt must not be planted in their hearts. Great is the burden and condemnation of any teacher who sows doubt in a trusting soul" (1938). Teachers were informed that the primary criterion for teaching was not scholastic achievement but a testimony, a conviction of the truthfulness of the gospel.

> No amount of learning, no amount of study, and no number of scholastic degrees, can take the place of this testimony, which is the *sine qua non* of the teacher in our Church school system. No teacher who does not have a real testimony of the truth of the Gospel as revealed to and believed by the Latter-day Saints, and a testimony of the Sonship and Messiahship of Jesus, and of the divine mission of Joseph Smith—including in all its reality the First Vision—has any place in the Church school system. If there be any such, and I hope and pray there are none, he should at once resign; if the Commissioner knows of any such and he does not resign, the Commissioner should request his resignation. The First Presidency expect this pruning to be made (ibid.).

Denying teachers in the church school system the right of academic freedom, Clark asserted twenty years later that "there is no academic freedom where spiritual matters

are concerned. The scriptures and the words of the prophets and the President of the Church control and are the
last word" (1958, 18). The general membership had received
a similar warning seven years earlier. The June 1945 *Ward
Teacher's Message* to all Mormons made matters explicit.

> When our leaders speak, the thinking has been done.
> When they propose a plan—it is God's plan. When they
> point the way, there is no other which is safe. When they
> give direction it should mark the end of controversy. God
> works in no other way. To think otherwise, without imme-
> diate repentance, may cost one his faith, may destroy his
> testimony, and leave him a stranger to the Kingdom of
> God ("A 1945 Perspective").

Mormon neo-orthodox theologians typically express
such anti-intellectualism in response to contemporary
Mormonism's cultural crisis. Chauncey Riddle—whose distinctions among physical, social, and intellectual persecution correspond roughly to my distinction between social
and cultural crises—argues that intellectual (cultural) challenges are the most serious. He wrote:

> Bad as physical and social persecution can be, I think
> that intellectual persecution is the most devastating. The
> former are by nature opposition from outside, and as
> such they may actually serve to strengthen the Church.
> But the intellectual attack also works within the Church.
> It divides and dilutes us when it comes from members
> (1975, 81).

If Riddle failed to perceive the enhanced social cohe-
sion and theological elaboration that may follow from institutional responses to heresy, he nonetheless identified the

intellectual challenge posed by secular education. Though Pearson and Yarn claimed that secular education is of limited value, Nibley even doubted its significance for ameliorating contemporary social problems.

> The way out is not to be found in the self-consoling merry-go-round of philosophy, the heroic self-dramatization of literature and art, or the self-reassuring posturings of science and scholarship. Men have tried everything for a long time and the idea that their condition has improved rests entirely on an imaginary reconstruction of the past devised to prove that very proposition. Not that the theory may not be right, but at present we just don't know; and for a world in as dire a predicament as ours, that can guarantee no long centuries of quiet research ahead and seems to need some quick and definite assistance if it is to survive at all, it might pay to consider what Mormon and Moroni have to offer (1969, 439–40).

Aware of the threat posed by secular education and more sophisticated in academic matters, Mormon neo-orthodox theologians during the 1960s and 1970s typically defended the divine character of the scriptures, repudiated biblical criticism, denied the theory of organic evolution, rejected the epistemology of science, and embraced revelation and the authority structure of the church as their criteria of truth. Thus, Pearson informed readers during the late 1960s that science had created a generation of "arrogant worshippers at the shrine of reason" (1967a) while secular education had produced the public school system to promulgate an atheistic "state religion" (1967c). People without the spirit of revelation, Yarn laments, are left to rely on "their own feeble reason" (1965, 170–80). "One of the great mistakes of the ages has always been that when men have lost revelation," according to Pearson, "they have turned to the human mind for understanding" (n.d.a, 2). In response to a critic, Pearson wrote:

> I think we must decide whether we accept the human mind of [sic] the divine mind. In other words, to what do you turn for your proofs? Or do you turn to the educated consensus? When it comes right down to it, there are only two epistemological systems possible to follow. One is revelation. The other is some consensus or another. Philosophers talk a great deal about the authoritarian method, the methodology of faith, intuition, cohesiveness, coherence, etc. God reveals from the whole to the part. Man reasons from the part to the whole. . . . Let first things be first, do you really believe with all your heart that the Book of Mormon came the way Joseph Smith said it did? (n.d.b, 3).

In *The World and the Prophets*, one of his polemics against nonrevelational approaches to knowledge, Nibley wrote:

> Science, philosophy, and common sense all have a right to their day in court. But the last word does not lie with them. Every time men in their wisdom have come forth with the last word, other words have promptly followed. The last word is a testimony of the gospel that comes only by direct revelation. Our Father in heaven speaks it, and if it were in perfect agreement with the science of today, it would surely be out of line with the science of tomorrow. Let us not, therefore, seek to hold God to the learned opinions of the moment when he speaks the language of eternity (1954, 122).

For Nibley, reason has been substituted for revelation, the

university for the church, the doctorate for the priesthood, and academic robes for the ordinances of the gospel (1960, 8).

Anti-intellectualism and authoritarianism have tended to permeate Mormon neo-orthodoxy, especially during the 1960s and into the early 1970s. Reacting to social differentiation and secularization, politically conservative Mormon leaders and neo-orthodox theologians found threatening the redefinition of America's role abroad, expansion of government with the development of the "welfare state," racial conflict, and secular education. These phenomena continue to underlay much of the cultural crisis confronting contemporary Mormonism.

PSYCHOLOGICAL AND THEOLOGICAL RESPONSES

The loss of meaning, purpose, and direction accompanying a cultural crisis provides an excellent context for religious experience, including revelation. It constitutes a "limit situation" in which cognitive perspectives and ordinary mental processes fail so that individuals consequently experience a profound sense of inadequacy, an inability to cope with the situation. The crisis itself, as was the case in Protestant neo-orthodoxy, can be both an important precondition for revelation and an element of it. Thus Emil Brunner argued that the imbalance occurring during a crisis is the "most important point of contact for the Gospel message" (1939, 234).

A poignant account of personal experience with such a crisis appeared in Chauncey Riddle's description of his graduate education. Encountering a professor who boasted about destroying faith, who attributed much of the evil in the world to religion, and who assigned all virtue in human progress to the development of reason and empiricism, Riddle remembered:

> Well, frankly I was devastated by that onslaught. There I was, a graduate student, well schooled in Latter-day Saint theology, happily Mormon all my life, a defender of the faith and successful sufferer under physical and social persecution—but devastated. He had made me realize that I did not have a personal testimony of revelation. All I had was an intellectual awareness of what others said about our religion. That realization shook me, for I realized that I might have been wrong.
>
> During the next few weeks I went through an experience for which I can think of only one word as a representation: hell. I was assailed by doubt, by fear, by loneliness; I began to wonder if I were sane. Through this time I kept two promises I made: I continued to go to Church, and I continued to read ten pages in the scriptures each night; but those things became an agony to me. And I prayed. Oh, how I prayed to know for myself if there were such a thing as personal revelation.
>
> Then—thanks to our good Master—it came. I began to feel something special in my breast. I began to recognize certain ideas that appeared in my mind as being different from my own thoughts. These new ideas told me how to interpret passages of scripture, how to understand things formerly incomprehensible to me, even to know the future. But I could tell the difference. Here was the iron rod. I had hold of it. The restored Gospel was true! (1975, 82).

Human inadequacy could hardly be more explicit than in Riddle's conclusion that "without Him I am nothing" (ibid.). And, of course, the sensations of contingency and powerlessness, which the crisis experience intensifies, become not only a statement of the human predicament but also an epiphany of the greatness of God. Even the desire to know God grows out of the awareness of one's contingency and powerlessness. "He begins to realize his own inadequacies as well as God's greatness," wrote Yarn, "and desires within his soul to draw near unto God and know the power and sweetness of his presence" (1965, 66).

Crisis also discloses the intensity of human guilt and reveals humans as sinful. Of salvation, Pearson wrote:

> There has to be down payment of a broken heart and a contrite spirit. Who has a broken heart and contrite spirit? One who is stripped of pride and selfishness. One who has come down in the depths of humility and prostrated himself before the Lord in mighty prayer and supplication. He has realized the awful guilt of his sins and has pled for the blood of Christ to be made a covering to shield him from the face of a just God. Such a one has made the down payment (1961, 169).

The mistrust of human reason and sensory experience, which can accompany the crisis situation, is obvious from our discussion of the Mormon neo-orthodox concept of human nature and its anti-intellectualism in the face of secular education. The neo-orthodox theologian celebrates human nonrationality in order to establish a premise for divine revelation, as well as to discredit critics. Since all

data must be interpreted from "a matrix of presuppositions," Riddle posited personal revelation as the foundation for human life. Ignoring the fact that whatever is experienced as revelation also rests upon similar presuppositions,
he wrote:

> So we are persecuted for personal revelation in a
> world that prides itself on "hard" evidence, on object-
> ivity, on the strength of consensus. As a philosopher of
> knowledge, I can only shake my head. For now I know
> and can prove that there is no such thing as evidence
> apart from a matrix of presuppositions, that objectivity
> is at best consensus, and that consensus is often but a
> public relations job. Every scientific system begins with
> unproved postulates. Every person founds his life on arti-
> cles of faith. But what a blessing to be able to ground
> faith on a rock—on personal daily revelation from our
> Savior (1975, 83).

Riddle's description of human nature clearly demonstrates
disdain for reason and sensory experience.

> Man . . . is cut off from knowing truth, and in the abso-
> lute sense, or final sense, he is cut off from determining
> by his own reason or by his own senses what the ulti-
> mate moral values of the universe are. . . . In this predic-
> ament the only way out that is reasonable and consis-
> tent is to seize upon the hand that is extended by the
> Lord and to be grateful to be lifted out of that predica-
> ment through the power of the gospel and the ordinances
> of the priesthood (n.d., 13).

Human beings cannot extricate themselves from this
predicament but must rely on an external force, for only
by the gracious act of an absolute God can they be saved.
However, this dependence upon external authority is

not limited to God. Indeed, the neo-orthodox theologians tend to express similar deference toward officials of the church. While Riddle would place his trust in the church rather than himself, Yarn, in a statement illustrating the psychological security typically accompaning submission to authority, claimed that "when one loves the Authorities and sustains the Authorities, he is given peace and satisfaction of spirit which can come in no other way than being in harmony with God's anointed ones" (1965, 86). And Pearson argued that one should follow the church even if he believes it to be wrong. Speaking of a person ideally committed to the church, he wrote:

> When the inspiration of the Lord to his prophets or other authorities has resulted in a decision, he will support it even if he feels it is wrong or there is a better way. If he can he will get an assurance through prayer that it is right. If he cannot get such an assurance he will support the Church policy because the Church is the hope of the world (1961, 232).

Such conviction of contingency and powerlessness encountered during crises gave rise to the profound nonrationality and authoritarianism embodied in much of Mormon neo-orthodoxy, especially as articulated during the 1960s. Reliance on external authority naturally follows from the incapacity to trust oneself. If the neo-orthodox theologians found in modern Mormonism's cultural crisis a revelation of human inadequacy, they also discovered the solution in an all-powerful God who could save them from their predicament. The very sensations experienced during a crisis became the fundamental elements of their theology, and feelings of contingency and powerlessness were generalized to describe the human condition. No longer limited to specific situations, they became defining qualities of human nature itself. The crisis experience was nothing less than a revelation of basic human nature. Given such inadequacy, dependence upon external authority is not surprising. A coherent theology integrating the doctrines of divine sovereignty, human depravity, and salvation by grace helped to reduce the anxieties of living in modernity.

RECENT DEVELOPMENTS.

CHAPTER 5.

Since the late 1970s, a new generation of theologians has taken up the banner of Mormon neo-orthodoxy. Usually more theologically sophisticated than their predecessors, they have concentrated primarily on the doctrines of human nature and salvation. The explosion of historical scholarship in Mormon studies during the past two decades has disclosed the essential Protestant flavor of the earliest Mormon beliefs and has provided an authentic foundation for Mormon neo-orthodox theology.

Much like the earliest Mormon converts, the latest neo-orthodox theologians rely primarily upon the Book of Mormon, not the story of Joseph Smith's first vision (Shipps 1985), for their doctrines of diety, human nature, and salvation. This emphasis on the Book of Mormon reinforces a trinitarian and absolute God, while a preoccupation with the first vision, a trademark of twentieth-century Mormonism, encourages a tritheistic and anthropocentric God. The post–1841 Nauvoo teachings of Joseph Smith on polytheism, eternal progression, necessity of human existence, exaltation, and the ultimate human destiny of godhood have become the building blocks of traditional Mormon theology, whereas the basic doctrines of the Book of Mormon, as the neo-orthodox theologians are inclined to argue, have, for most modern Mormons, been relegated to the periphery.

As a pluralistic metaphysics became the philosophical foundation of Mormon doctrine, the concepts of human nature and salvation contained in the Book of Mormon disappeared from traditional Mormon theology. Perhaps the least representative of the Book of Mormon pronouncements on the human condition has become its most celebrated quote among traditional Mormons, namely: "Adam fell that men might be, and men are that they might have joy" (2 Ne. 2:25).

HUMAN NATURE

If the way most Mormons today use 2 Nephi 2:25 distorts the basic Book of Mormon concept of human nature, it is nonetheless consistent with their denial of the classical Christian doctrines of original sin and human depravity and their affirmation of humanity's necessary existence and innate goodness. That the new generation of neo-orthodox theologians recognize that most Mormons accept the traditional Mormon doctrine of human nature is obvious from the "resistance" they report to their own neo-orthodox doctrine (see P. Toscano 1983, 91; Allred 1983, 13; Olson, 1984, 21; Voros 1985, 1). In distinguishing between "humanistic" and "redemptive" Mormonism, J. Frederic Voros, for instance, contends that "the popular hegemony" of humanistic Mormonism (his term for traditional Mormonism) "is nearly complete" (ibid.). Not supris-

ingly, he and other Mormon neo-orthodox theologians contend that this popular view denies the basic doctrines of
the Book of Mormon.

Beginning with a premise of human depravity, the
new Mormon neo-orthodox theologians proclaim a Pauline
theology which they identify with the Book of Mormon. A
typical list of supporting passages includes Mosiah 3:19—
the "natural man is an enemy to God, and has been from
the fall of Adam"; Alma 42:6–12—"fallen man" has became
"carnal, sensual, and devilish, by nature," which "man had
brought upon himself because of his own disobedience";
and Ether 3:2—"we are unworthy before thee; because of
the fall our natures have become evil continually" (see P.
Toscano 1983; Olsen 1984; Voros 1978; 1985). If the Book
of Mormon teaches anything about human nature, they
insist, it is that human beings are "lost," "fallen,"
"corrupt," "helpless," and "condemned" before God. It is
clear to these theologians that the Fall transformed human
nature leaving human beings helpless.

But what does it mean to be fallen? Is this comparable to classical Christian doctrines of original sin? While
the traditional Catholic view holds that the Fall resulted in
the withdrawal of supernatural grace, the typical Protestant view assumes that the Fall corrupted human nature;
both share the judgment that all humanity are in a state of
sin. Remember that traditional Mormonism emphatically
denies the doctrine of original sin, proclaiming the inherent goodness of human nature, and regards the Fall as a

necessary condition for the ultimate exaltation of humanity. While the Fall introduced mortality and separated human beings from the immediate presence of God, it did not transform human nature but established conditions for the further development of human potential. To neo-orthodox Mormons, on the other hand, the Fall definitely transformed human nature. Their position most resembles the Protestant view described above and least resembles traditional Mormon doctrine.

Human depravity is inextricably bound to the doctrine of original sin in Reformation and neo-orthodox Protestantism. For these theologians, original sin is a state or condition—human depravity—from which specific acts are "fruits" or consequences of sin. In the most extreme formulation, human beings are incapable of doing good; they can only sin. Though he rejected the static quality of the Reformation doctrines of original sin, Emil Brunner, a Protestant neo-orthodox theologian, preserved Luther's and Calvin's fundamental "insight" by arguing that whenever humans act they act against God (1939, 148). Thus, sin is both a state of being and a behavior.

Though less extreme than these Protestants, the recent Mormon neo-orthodox writers, with the possible exception of Janice Allred, seem to espouse a position of depravity that implicitly entails a doctrine of original sin. If they seldom use the term "original sin," they freely speak of depravity and fallen human nature. Noting that his Mormon audiences "hardly ever" give him an "opportunity to explain that the words 'depraved' and 'fallen nature' " do not refer to "bad conduct," Paul Toscano observes that "depravity refers to mankind's essential corruptibility, to the fact that man is born of corruptible seed, lives in a fallen state, and is subject to the powers of deterioration and destruction" (1983, 91). And Donald P. Olsen writes that "humankind requires grace because they are in a lost, fallen, and corrupt state, incapable of regaining God's presence without divine intervention" (1984, 21).

Voros reverses the aphorism of traditional Mormonism used to affirm the fundamental goodness of human nature—"As man now is, God once was; as God now is, man may become"—to establish human depravity—"as man is, *Cain* once was; as Cain is, man may become" (1979, 4). Speaking of sin as "in our very natures," he reminds readers that sinfulness is not "temporarily superimposed" on one: "It *is* your true self" (ibid.). In fact, the doctrine that "man is 'fallen' or 'depraved' " and consequently "powerless to extricate himself from his fallen condition" is so crucial that it constitutes the "single teaching" by which "true Christianity can be distinguished from all other religions" (P. Toscano, 1983, 90).

The writings of these theologians project an ambiance much more characteristic of Protestant than Mormon theology, as the following quotation from Toscano suggests:

> The word and works of Jesus Christ may best be seen against the dark background of man's depravity or fallen nature. Men cannot be expected to rejoice in sal-

vation if they do not see clearly the peril from which they are saved, if they do not know the sort of prison it is from which they have been liberated, if they are unaware of the severity of the sentence that is passed upon them and from which they are pardoned, if they are ignorant of the fatal disease which infects them and from which they are cured by the marvelous healing light of Christ Jesus, who is the light and life of the world. For this reason the prophets of Christ have not only included this doctrine in their preaching, but have sometimes *begun* their explanations of the gospel with descriptions of man's depravity, sin, and malice (1983, 90).

Even so, this position is less extreme than that of Reformation and neo-orthodox Protestants. None of these Mormon theologians accepts the doctrine of total depravity. Associated primarily with Calvin, total depravity means that not only can human beings do no good, they are incapable of desiring good. Depravity was so profound for Calvin that even human will was corrupt. Indeed, to assume that one's desires and actions might be in accordance with God was a profoundly arrogant claim revealing the very depth of human sinfulness. While Mormon neoorthodox theologians may disagree slightly among themselves regarding the "goodness" of human action, they appear to share the judgment that the will itself is not depraved. This, of course, is not to say that there are not human beings who desire to do evil, but it does mean that one can desire to do good. Thus, Paul Toscano suggests that humans are not necessarily "set on evil" or incapable of "pleasing" God as long as they do his will. However, they are sufficiently corrupt to be unable to do anything significant to save themselves (1983, 74–78). While we are free to choose good or evil, Voros insists that "free will alone provides no escape from the Fall, since man tends to exercise his freedom to satisfy his own will" (1985, 5).

As in traditional Mormonism, the freedom to choose between good and evil justifies the judgment of God (P. Toscano 1983, 100), but unlike traditional Mormonism it does not imply a doctrine of salvation by merit. It simply enables humans to obey God. An "apparent contradiction" between freedom and authority in the Mormon religion, according to Paul Toscano, "evaporates when we understand that freedom is the foundation of obedience to authority." Without the choice, compliance is oppression not obedience (1983, 101).

In addition to affirming free will in this way, Mormon neo-orthodox theologians distinguish between "universal sin" and "personal" or "individual" sin to reject the idea of total depravity. Though these theologians abandon the traditional Mormon concept of "actual sin," the notion of personal sin, at least for Allred, seems to offer a compromise between traditional Mormon and classical Protestant doctrines (1983). Allred defines sin in traditional Mormon terms, as a violation of a divine commandment, but believes that the traditional definition of the "mortal state"—a condition of moral imperfection—cannot explain the inevitability of sin. By shifting the discussion away from innate qualities, an assumption of human depravity, she posits three characteristics of the "fallen condition" that make sin inevitable: first, commandments sometimes conflict with one another which means that even the establishing of priorities will require that a lesser commandment be violated; second, human finitude means that our egocentricity, as well as lack of knowledge and power, necessarily limit our capacity to do good and avoid sin; and, finally, the solidarity of humankind, which in part includes the cultural values and prejudices shared with others of our group and society, not only shape choices and behavior but remove some responsibility from individuals as they act in terms of those values and prejudices. Since these universal characteristics of the human condition guarantee the inevitability of sin, Allred has formulated "a Mormon concept of original sin" (ibid.).

If other Mormon neo-orthodox theologians define sin as the violation of a commandment of God, they nevertheless also conceive of the individual "sin" as a product of a "sinful state." In this sense, their concept of sin varies little from the classical Protestant notion that acts are "fruits" or consequences of original sin (Voros 1978; Olsen 1984). Consider Toscano's distinction between depravity and sin:

> Depravity then refers to man's innate corruptibility and his present subjection to the law of entropy, of physicial and spiritual decay and deterioration.
> The term "sin," however, refers to man's acts and omissions that run counter to God's will and authority. Depravity refers merely to the corruption in man's nature;

sin refers to man's misdeeds that arise out of that corrupt nature. Depravity is the cause, sin is the effect.
Depravity exists within each of us like a disease; our sins
are its outward symptoms. The disease is still in the latent
stage in little children so that symptoms do not surface
at first. But eventually the depravity will be exposed by
misdeeds, errors in judgment, and incontinence without.
Sin is the manifestation of our corrupt natures, our
human, fallen natures, our depravity (1983, 92).

Given the emphasis on depravity, the little attention devoted to the necessary existence of human beings by
these Mormon neo-orthodox writers is not surprising. The
assumption that intelligence, the essence of an individual,
exists necessarily underlies the optimism of traditional Mormon doctrines of human nature and salvation (exaltation).
The moral nature of human beings and their freedom and
autonomy are often grounded in the uncreated intelligence.
Though he would hardly attribute these qualities to
uncreated intelligences, Paul Toscano indicates that
humanity's necessary existence may mean that at some point
"individuals were able to exist independent of the life powers that come from God" (1983, 4).

However, the occasional references to intelligences
among other neo-orthodox theologians appear to diminish
the significance of necessary being. Allred observes that to
"be uncreated is not necessarily to be essentially good"
(1983, 14), and Margaret Toscano suggests that Joseph
Smith's statement that "our intelligences were 'co-equal with
God himself' "—which, it should be remembered, was inter-

preted historically to mean co-eternal or uncreated—implies
"undifferentiated wholeness." She recalls "a statement of
John Taylor's to the effect that, as intelligences, we were
somehow part of the mind of God, and 'struck from the
fire of his eternal blaze' " (1986, 8). It is not clear if she
means to imply that a lack of differentiation destroys human
autonomy, but her reference to intelligences as "part of the
mind of God" ultimately establishes the contingency, not
the necessity, of human existence. In fact, such was the
intent of certain Mormon neo-orthodox theologians of the
previous generation in asserting that intelligences constituted an "undifferentiated mass" (see chap. 4).

SALVATION

Nothing distinguishes the recent neo-orthodoxy from
traditional Mormonism and, to a lesser extent, the earlier
generation of Mormon neo-orthodox theologians more than
the explicitness of its Pauline theology. The preoccupation
among new Mormon neo-orthodox theologians with the
grace of Christ, justification, sanctification, and the futil-
ity of works exceeds anything produced by their predecessors. This "redemptive Mormonism" is different from
"humanistic Mormonism," to use Voros's categories, by its
emphasis on the Fall, rebirth, and redemption by grace;
scepticism of human effort; and insistence on the active
role of God in the salvation process compared to humanistic Mormonism's emphasis on the inherent goodness of
human nature, human potential, and human effort; skepti-

cism of reliance upon God; and insistance on salvation by merit. Redemptive Mormonism is theocentric while humanistic Mormonism is anthrocentric. "Redemptive Mormonism promises transformation" while "humanistic Mormonism promises reformation" (Voros 1985, 1). Of course, Voros's distinction between redemptive and humanistic Mormonism, both of which profess to be orthodox, is essentially my distinction between neo-orthodox and traditional Mormonism.

Voros's contention that the "popular hegemony of the humanistic view is nearly complete" (ibid.) would seem to underscore the continuing dominance of traditional Mormonism. Thus Donald P. Olsen asserts that "few doctrines are as well supported in scripture yet as thoroughly misunderstood by Latter-day Saints as the doctrine of the grace of Christ" (1984, 21). Indeed, when he continues by noting that Mormons typically assume that grace refers to the "gift of the resurrection," he implicitly identifies one of the reasons traditional Mormonism was concerned with exaltation rather than salvation. Essentially subscribing to a doctrine of universal salvation, in which only the Sons of Perdition would be excluded from the resurrection and a degree of glory in heaven, traditional Mormonism proclaimed exaltation—a process in which individuals could attain godhood—as its mission (see chap. 3). And the path to exaltation was largely one of moral development or, to use Voros's language, "reformation."

The recent neo-orthodoxy, in contrast, virtually

ignores exaltation and concentrates instead on salvation. The latter becomes the major theological problem because of the profound discontinuity between divine and human natures. While divine justice requires perfection, human depravity precludes it. Consequently, humanity stands "condemned before divine justice" (P. Toscano 1983, 2). Only perfection can pay the debt of imperfection. Being merciful as well as just, Jesus Christ took upon himself the sins of the world so that depraved, helpless sinners might live. "He carried our cross to Calvary, not his. We deserved crucifixion, not he" (ibid., 75). Thus, the redemption of humanity was beyond itself. "The Lord decided not to leave these important achievements to us. That is why the gospel is such 'good news.' Our redemption from death and hell was too vital to be trusted to us. God does the work of salvation almost totally on his own" (ibid.).

This is, of course, the doctrine of salvation by grace. The law of justification involves the "attributing of Christ's righteousness to the undeserving sinner so that he appears righteous to God" (Olsen 1984, 22). Since Christ has "fully paid" for sins, "the justified sinner is not accountable for them" (ibid., 23). Grace is a gift from God, not something earned or deserved. However, the fact that "grace is an undeserved favor freely given does not mean justification is unconditional" (ibid.). On the contrary, one must believe in Christ, "believe that justification is by the grace of Christ" (ibid.). Redemption comes through the four basic principles of the gospel: faith, repentance, baptism, and reception of the Holy Ghost.

Yet, one should not assume that this requires significant human effort. "These simple actions," writes Paul Toscano, "amount to nothing more than holding still and letting God work in us spiritually" (1983, 11). Indeed, the act of faith itself is not really a human endeavor but rather a product of divine grace (ibid., 53). Olson writes that "even the ability and motivation to have faith, repent, be baptized, and receive the Holy Ghost must also come by grace" (1984, 23). Consequently, the eventual espousal of a doctrine of total depravity, where even the will is corrupt, may become too seductive to resist for theologians who assume that "the carnal man cannot repent unless God wills it" (ibid.).

Obviously, these theologians repudiate traditional Mormonism's doctrine of salvation by merit. Human efforts are sufficiently tainted so that any reform, which is dependent upon human will, must fail; redemption requires supernatural intervention. Even conservative Mormon authorities, such as the late apostle Bruce McConkie, are criticized for identifying the idea of "salvation by 'grace alone without works'" as the 'second greatest heresy' of Christendom" and assuming that "justification 'becomes operative in the life of an individual only on conditions of personal righteousness'" (ibid., 21–22). To the neo-orthodox, works are irrelevant. Justification occurs only "when we rely 'wholly upon the merits' of Christ—not upon our personal works or worthiness'' (ibid., 23). Sanctification, which the neo-orthodox use to indicate a state of righteousness or holiness, is also a product of grace. It does not, according to Olsen, come ''as a result of personal merit, but is the means by which personal merit is obtained'' (ibid.); and Voros argues that ''the Book of Mormon clearly teaches that man cannot earn salvation'' and ''even our own good works are God's gift; if they are not, they are not truly good'' (1985, 7–8). Thus, faith, which comes from hearing or reading the word of God, precedes works. ''Good works come in later. For it is the Spririt that attends the faithful that reveals to them what good works to do, to whom, and when'' (P. Toscano 1983, 58). Good works are a consequence of grace, not a cause of it, and their purpose is to bring people to Christ and glorify God.

This means, then, that the traditional Mormon notion of repentance is simply moral reform. For the neo-orthodox, this position is a concession to the false doctrine of works. Repentance requires a divine transformation of human nature, not the taking of either ''baby'' or ''giant'' steps; it requires ''getting one's feet planted on the right way'' (P. Toscano 1983, 11). It results in a ''covenant'' with God ''to exchange our corruption for his incorruption; to put off our human nature and take upon ourselves his divine nature; to trade our state of powerlessness and helplessness for the gift of the Holy Spirit'' (ibid., 25). In short, we must all be born again.

The Mormon neo-orthodox doctrine of salvation is summarized by Olsen as follows:

> Those who truly have the grace of Christ have faith unto repentance, receive baptism and the Holy Ghost, are justified, are in the process of becoming sanctified, have received salvation from sin, and may have received eternal life. These blessings will be theirs so long as they do not fall from grace by trusting in good works or by attempting to earn, merit, or deserve these blessings. Those who continue in grace will someday stand before God where Christ will plead their case saying to the Father, "I am their righteousness; I have paid justice for their sins." Then God will see only the good works of Christ and say to them, "Enter thou into the joy of the Lord" (1984, 25).

GOD

Though these new Mormon theologians seem less concerned with the concept of God than with the doctrines of human nature and salvation, their position on the classical attributes of omniscience, omnipotence, and omnipresence is evident. A preoccupation with Christ's perfection and divine justice naturally follows from an emphasis on human failure and the gift of grace (see Olsen 1984; P. Toscano 1983). However, few of these theologians have thus far attempted to reconcile elements of the traditional Mormon concept of God with their theology, leaving them with unresolved philosophical and theological contradictions.

The traditional Protestant insistence on the otherness of God follows from its doctrine of the depravity of human nature. It is this discontinuity between divine and human natures that enables divine grace to reconcile fallen man. Only a sovereign God, whose perfection and permanence is ensured, can save human beings. When writing about human nature and salvation, recent Mormon neo-orthodox theologians have apparently consented to these assumptions. Paul Toscano insists that Jesus Christ was "perfect from the outset" (1983, 2), and Voros acknowledges the Book of Mormon's "unchangeable and eternal God" (1985, 12). Voros's uneasy reconciliation of the God of the Book of Mormon (who "is the same, yesterday, today, and forever") with the God of Joseph Smith's 1844 King Follett discourse ("who was once man") cannot preserve the values of divine sovereignty. To limit the Book of Mormon to the "chronological boundaries" of human existence while assuming that the King Follett discourse refers to human pre-mortal and post-mortal existence does not eliminate the contradiction between a progressive and an unchanging God (see ibid., 12–13).

The absoluteness of God cannot be maintained simply by assuming that God is absolute at one point in time and not at another. To formulate this, as Voros does, as a chronological problem, is to place God within rather than beyond time. This may be consistent with the pluralistic metaphysics underlying Mormon theology and the King Follett Discourse—which assumes that God exists within an environment of uncreated matter, time, space, and intelligence—but it also means that God is necessarily finite, that he exists within an environment over which he lacks complete control. Assuming this, it is impossible to posit the omniscience, omnipotence, and omnipresence of God—to proclaim that "God is the same yesterday, today, and forever." Such assertions deny the meaning of these concepts.

With the doctrine of the *ex nihilo* creation, classical Christianity placed God beyond everything. Only he existed necessarily, all else—space, time, and humanity itself—being his creation, existed contingently. The total otherness of God, his perfection, enables him to redeem and promise eternal life to his fallen creatures. Whatever one may think of this theology, it is consistent: A totally other God is necessary to save corrupt human beings through his gift of grace. Mormon neoorthodox theologians, whose doctrines of human nature and salvation have a basic coherence, are forced into a contradictory position in regards to their concept of deity by their acceptance of Mormon metaphysics. Insisting that God is "NOT totally other," Paul Toscano's accommodation of Mormon and classical Christian concepts of God is not adequately reconciled. He writes:

> For us God is thus: paradoxical, supreme, holy, anthropomorphic, male and female, omnipotent, omniscient, omnipresent, and omnibenevolent; loving, caring, creating, forgiving, and intervening—a Divine One, at once on a throne and yet in and through all things, whose infinitude is beyond finite comprehension, but who is known through his Only Begotten Son, Jesus Christ (1986, 19).

Margaret Toscano presents an interesting explanation of Mormon cosmology by using a model based on the psychological theories of Swiss pyschiatrist Carl Jung. She interprets pre-mortal, mortal, and post-mortal existence as movement through four stages, from "undifferentiated wholeness" to integrative wholeness. The latter, which constitutes the reconciliation of opposites, is comparable to post-mortal existence in which the controlling deity is neither God the Father nor God the Mother "but the Divine Couple, locked in an erotic embrace" (1986, 17).

While this attempt to integrate the sexual differentiation inherent in traditional Mormonism's concept of God has interesting possibilities,[1] it suffers from the same incon-

---

[1]Toscano's image of the "Divine Couple locked in erotic embrace" is perhaps the most promising avenue for addressing sexual inequality in Mormon theology. I have argued (1986a) that the nineteenth-century Mormon idea of the family provided a basis for Mormonism's universalistic impulses. The logical conclusion of Mormon conceptions of the eternal nature of the family, genealogical activity, and the rituals surrounding the dead is the incorporation of the entire human species into one huge kinship structure. By insisting that sexual differentiation, as well as behavior, survives death, traditional Mormonism assumes that this differentiation is inherent in reality itself. A Father-in-Heaven requires the existence of a Mother-in-Heaven, and Mormon references to both are not metaphorical. Since the differences implicit in sexual differentiation cannot be transcended, Mormon universalism depends upon a *union* of male and female. Tangentially, this theological predicament may be one reason why Mormonism is not receptive to feminist and gay social movements. By separating sex from procreation and celebrating unmarried life styles, feminist and gay people challenge the Mormon vision of the human destiny (1986a, 302-303).

In contrast, the terms "Fatherhood of God" and "brotherhood of man" in the Christian tradition are masculine metaphors for estab-

sistencies plaguing Voros's and Paul Toscano's doctrines of deity. One simply cannot proclaim that God is absolute and retain traditional Mormon metaphysics. In fact, none of the new Mormon neo-orthodox theologians reconciles divine absolutism with Mormon metaphysics any more convincingly than their predecessors, though they achieve greater coherence in their doctrines of human nature and salvation. The coherence of the latter, however, is accomplished only by moving even closer to Reformation and Protestant neo-orthodox theologies and further away from traditional Mormonism.

---

lishing human equality; they identify a universal condition of human contingency. However, Christian universalism rests ultimately on a deity who is beyond distinctions. Distinctions such as sexual differentiation are products of the Creation and disappear in the classical Christian conception of heaven. Thus, the universalism and equality of Christianity requires the transcending of distinctions, not the "union of opposites."

CONCLUSION.

M ormon neo-orthodox theology is a post-World War II response to the twentieth-century accommodation of Mormonism to American society. Traditional Mormon metaphysics, the affirmation of the temporal world, and a preoccupation over conflict with non-Mormons and the federal government mitigated much of the impact of secularization in the nineteenth century. During the second and third decades of the twentieth century, some Mormon intellectuals and church leaders attempted to integrate Mormon theology and modern science. These efforts reinforced the theological synthesis of traditional Mormonism, including its concept of a finite God, its optimistic assessment of human nature, and its doctrine of salvation by merit. Contemporary Mormonism, especially since the 1950s, has assumed a more ambivalent posture, and the anti-intellectual and authoritarian reactions of some Mormon leaders and theologians to secularization challenge the synthesis of traditional Mormon theology.

In response to secularization, Mormon neo-orthodox theologians have embraced some fundamental doctrines of Protestant neo-orthodoxy. The latter's affirmation of the sovereignty of God, the depravity of human nature, and the necessity of salvation by grace was a conscious effort to recapture the essential meaning of Reformation theology in lieu of the "sterility" of liberal Protestantism. These doctrines typically reflected the sensations experienced during neo-orthodox crises with liberalism and modernity. For Protestant neo-orthodox theologians, the secularization of culture constituted a critical situation in which feelings of human inadequacy and helplessness led to a theology emphasizing human contingency, the absoluteness of God, and the necessity of divine intervention to save a helpless humanity.

The encounter with secularization produced a similar cultural crisis for Mormon neo-orthodox theologians. Experienced as a "limit situation," where ordinary intellectual and psychological means of coping breakdown, the individual becomes profoundly aware of his limitations. He feels inadequate and helpless. The only way out appears to be to grasp a power beyond himself. These reactions combine with sensations of contingency and helplessness to become the social and psychological foundation of the doctrines of divine sovereignty, human depravity, and salvation by grace. Indeed, this theology crystallizes the basic elements of the neo-orthodox religious experience. As the crisis is a revelation of the human predicament and the divine/human relationship, neo-orthodox theology is a generalization of those sensations encountered during the crisis.

The appearance of a neo-orthodox movement poses some important implications for traditional Mormon theology. Of special significance is the Mormon neo-orthodox concept of revelation. By contrasting revelation with reason and empiricism, the neo-orthodox theologian shares much with the Christian tradition in general while apparently denying the spirit of traditional Mormonism. A subtle shift in the meaning of revelation occurs, for example, when Hugh Nibley (1973) reminds us that the "absurdity" of the Mormon denial of the priesthood to blacks prior to 1978 constituted evidence for its divinity, when Glenn Pearson and Reid Bankhead (1962, 67) assure us that any conflict between two propositions must be apparent, not real, if they appear in the scriptures, and when Paul Toscano celebrates the "paradoxical" nature of God (1986) and conceives of his own reason as the "voice of the devil" (1983, 59). These are concepts of revelation that, I believe, deny the rationality of traditional Mormonism, which has little sympathy for paradoxical revelation that "baffles the intellect." Such a notion depends on the otherness of God and the depravity of humanity—on the profound discontinuity between creator and creature—and evidently requires that religion, as well as religious experience, be nonrational. For only by abandoning reason and the human intellect can one fully appreciate the Incomprehensible God and the "absurd," or paradoxical, gospel.

But God is neither incomprehensible nor is the gospel paradoxical for traditional Mormonism. Nor is revelation antithetical to reason. In fact, Mormon revelation is rational; its purpose is to make matters more intelligible. It proposes to clarify, not to confuse, to solve problems and answer questions, not to indicate that problems are illusory and questions illegitimate. Mormon revelation is explicit. When traditional Mormons tell of God revealing himself to Joseph Smith, for example, God tries neither to baffle the boy's intellect nor to demonstrate his paradoxical nature. God was not something so large that he could fill the immensity of space and yet so small that he could dwell within the heart of a man. God, for Joseph Smith, was a person, with a tangible body, with spatial and temporal dimensions. He was comprehensible, not something beyond the logical grasp or understanding of human beings. If differences between God and humanity were evident, they were not so significant that Smith could not intellectually apprehend the divine message.

Though Mormon neo-orthodoxy challenges the rational nature of traditional Mormon revelation, its position is not yet as extreme as that of Protestant neo-orthodoxy. The preoccupation with God as "totally other" and human nature as corrupt has led some Protestant neo-orthodox theologians to differentiate revelation from religion. While revelation is God's gracious act of reaching downward to save depraved humanity, religion is arrogant humanity's attempt to become God. The former is praised; the latter is damned (cf. Tillich 1955, 1-10). Wicked, helpless human beings cannot legitimately reach for God. Such action is the epitome of pride, arrogance, and blasphemy. It is proof of original sin. Any action—any divine/human relationship—must be initiated by God. If Mormon neo-orthodox theologians have thus far avoided this position, their concept of revelation may ultimately force them to the same conclusion (see Edwards 1980, 49).

Related to this concept of revelation is the distrust among many Mormon neo-orthodox theologians of rationalism and empiricism. Yet reason and sensory experience are crucial in traditional Mormon thought. Not only are they useful to human beings in their earthly sojourn, they are essential in order to acquire knowledge necessary for godhood. Mormonism's pluralistic metaphysics, which assumes an orderly reality based upon eternal natural, moral, and spiritual laws, implies a mastery of these laws for human beings to realize their destiny. Only when learning at their fullest capacity are Latter-day Saints living in accordance with their religion.

This faith in the human intellect is consistent with the emphasis on secular education characteristic of Mormonism. Traditional Mormonism went beyond classical Christianity in the direction of Judaism to affirm the basic goodness of the world, the body, and the mind. It did not need the classical Christian distinction between sacred and secular since much that had previously been considered secular was now sacred. Even human beings were uncreated entities capable of becoming gods. Mormon theology thereby denied the old discontinuities between God and his "creation."

That this orientation was compatible with the belief

that education helps solve problems and brings human beings closer to godhood is apparent in the exegeses of Mormon scriptures proclaiming that the "glory of God is intelligence" and that "men are saved no faster than they gain knowledge." Insofar as a knowledge of matter and physical properties is necessary to organize and control worlds, some body of knowledge equivalent to physics and chemistry is apparently necessary for exaltation. Insofar as a knowledge of physiology and human behavior is necessary for an understanding of human nature, some body of knowledge equivalent to biology and psychology is also apparently necessary for exaltation. And so on. This concept of education, which follows from traditional Mormon metaphysics and theology, provides the basis for the belief that "the gospel embraces all truth."

Much of Mormon neo-orthodoxy seems to challenge this faith in education. A significant consequence of the distrust of reason and sensory experience, and the narrow concept of the knowledge essential for "salvation," of many neo-orthodox theologians represents an anti-intellectualism which, I believe, could radically affect Mormonism's commitment to education. Without its traditional faith in the human intellect, Mormonism could become increasingly susceptible to emotional excesses and superstition. Indeed, Mormons may be more likely to withdraw from modern secular society and become increasingly preoccupied with their own parochial problems. These are possible consequences of an inordinate anti-intellectualism.

The nonrationality of neo-orthodox theologians can only be reinforced by recent statements from several church leaders. As top officials of the Mormon church, Ezra Taft Benson, Bruce R. McConkie, Boyd K. Packer, Neal A. Maxwell, Gordon B. Hinckley, Dallin H. Oaks, and Russell M. Nelson have all publicly assumed positions that can only be regarded as anti-intellectual (see Bergera and Priddis 1985, 86-92, 411n83; Packer 1981; Maxwell 1979b). Apostle Oaks, for example, declared in 1985 that Mormons should not criticize their leaders even if that criticism is true (1985, 25), while Apostle Nelson suggested that, "in some instances, the merciful companion to truth is *silence*. Some truths are better left unsaid" (1985, 8; emphasis in original). And in highly publicized speeches, apostles Benson and McConkie advocated uncritical obedience to present church authorities even when the latter are in conflict with previous leaders (Benson 1980; McConkie 1978; McConkie 1982). Recent efforts to circumscribe scholarship and intellectual inquiry have been apparent in the responses of apostles Benson and Packer to the work of Mormon historians, in the church's officially barring some Mormons from speaking at church gatherings, and in calling others before local church officials to account for their writings (see Bergera and Priddis 1985, 86-92; *Salt Lake Tribune*, 23, 26 May 1983). While these and similar actions tend to reinforce the apparent nonrationality and authoritarianism of neo-orthodox theologians, their impact on Mormon intellectual endeavors remains to be seen.

Such sentiments could inhibit the resolution of what many theologians consider to be philosophical difficulties in Mormon theology. Because of their concept of God as omnipotent, omniscient, and/or omnipresent, some neo-orthodox theologians are hesitant to explore traditional Mormonism's finite God as a potential solution to the problem of evil. Sterling M. McMurrin (1965), Paul M. Edwards (1980; 1984), and Blake T. Ostler (1984) have underscored the value of a finite God while limiting both divine power and knowledge. Traditional Mormon theology, according to Edwards, provides "the best potential theodicy in the Western world" (1980, 49). If traditional Mormonism enjoys an enviable position with its "potential theodicy," it may still possess too much theological baggage to develop a logically consistent theodicy. The very attempt to address this difficulty with any degree of sophistication becomes even more problematic, however, in view of the anti-intellectualism encouraged by neo-orthodoxy.

Mormon and Protestant neo-orthodoxy generally differ on the matter of social ethics. While Mormon neo-orthodox theologians—with few exceptions, the most significant of whom is Nibley—tend to espouse a conservative political ideology with a superficial social critique, the strength of Protestant neo-orthodoxy derives from its analysis of social problems and critique of Protestant liberalism. With their naively optimistic conceptions of human nature, both religious and secular liberals, according to Reinhold Niebuhr, have reduced complex social problems to a simplistic human psychology (1932; see also Kenney 1980). Liberals typically explained the inequalities among races, classes, and nations as products of prejudice and misperception, having their origins in ignorance. Since human beings are moral and rational, the solution to social inequity was to develop compassion and moral goodwill by increasing human reason and knowledge. As the emerging social sciences provided the requisite knowledge, education would become the process of dissemination. Together they would ensure social progress.

Niebuhr rejected this liberal concept of human nature. Though humans were moral in possessing the capacity to place another's interest above their own, they were also immoral, or self-centered. Indeed, it was this preoccupation with themselves—this egoism—that made the Reformation doctrine of original sin so appealing. Nowhere, according to Niebuhr, had human selfishness and pride been so perceptively acknowledged. While his position was not as extreme as those of Barth and Brunner, Niebuhr found human beings far more immoral than moral. Though capable of morality, people act immorally.

But even more important was the liberals' failure to distinguish between individual and collective human nature. Because of their moral capacity, individuals dealing with one another in interpersonal settings may suppress self-interest as new information is presented to them or appeals are made to their sense of compassion. However, human collectivities, whether groups, classes, or nations, will not act morally. Not only are collectivities organized to protect self-interest, but, ironically, they even exploit individual altruism. Patriotism and war show how the sacrifice of individuals for their society is transmuted into collective self-interest. As an individual puts the interests of others within his society above his own, the society uses his sacrifice and energy to further its own selfish ends. Similarly the relations between groups, races, and classes within a society form a mosaic of collective interests.

To Niebuhr social inequalities are not a product of prejudice and ignorance, but are a result of differences in power associated with collective interests. Indeed, prejudice is a rationalization of social inequality. Reason, which is as likely to be a slave of the passions as to liberate the mind, is typically employed in the preservation of interests and the elaboration of prejudice rather than the betterment of society. Consequently, education may simply teach privileged groups more devious ways of protecting their interests. Though he did believe that an appeal to reason and moral goodwill offered some hope at the interpersonal level, Niebuhr believed that it was purely utopian to expect results at the intergroup level. Privileged classes, as Martin Luther King, Jr., would later learn from both Niebuhr and personal experience, do not—even when made aware of their privileges—abandon them willingly. Only strategies that empower weaker parties have any hope of producing social justice. Thus Niebuhr prophetically concluded, in 1932, that American blacks could expect social justice only by abandoning hope in the moral goodwill and reasonableness of their oppressors and by adopting the nonviolent, direct confrontation strategies of Ghandi. Only coercive tactics, in this case nonviolent ones, promised any success.

Niebuhr's critique of religious and secular liberalism provided neo-orthodox Protestants with an excellent framework in which to debate the question of social justice and to develop appropriate strategies for the creation of a more just society. While they had lost confidence that human beings could bring about the good society—the Kingdom of God on earth—they at least retained hope in a more just society as a potential human creation. However, even the latter would not become a reality through the naively optimistic strategies of liberalism. Change required a new social analysis.

Among Mormon neo-orthodox theologians, only Hugh Nibley has thus far expressed similar concerns with equality and the development of a social ethic based on premises other than those of laissez-faire economics. Using the Book of Mormon, which he claimed is directed primarily towards the Latter-day Saints, Nibley denounced inequalities in wealth and the preoccupation with power that characterizes contemporary Mormon and American society. He saw a prophetic message to the modern church in Book of Mormon warnings about the "accumulation of wealth," the appearance of "ambitious men," and a special concern with "power and gain" (1969, 391). While the most serious consequence of wealth, "according to the Book of Mormon, is the inequality it begets in any society," such inequality "is sometimes even its purpose." Mormons especially need to guard against accumulation of wealth, with its attendant inequalities, because of the unique susceptibility of "wealth oriented societies" to seek "moral justification in a display of religious piety." The latter, according to Nibley, is a profound insight of the Book of Mormon (ibid., 394-95).

Reminiscent of Michael Harrington's *The Other America*, a book partly responsible for the 1960s' "War on Poverty," Nibley argued that affluence results in the invisibility of the poor. The preoccupation with power and wealth seduces people into forgetting about others, so poverty becomes a fact of life. People merely suffer the poor, in the words of the Book of Mormon, "to pass by you, and notice them not." Nibley wrote, "They just don't exist. The guilty conscience, or rather, the guilty subconscious, is hypersensitive to criticism . . . and reacts vigorously to it, denouncing the critic as 'a false prophet . . . a sinner, and of the devil' " (ibid., 395). Moreover, the message of the Book of Mormon is clear: poverty must be eradicated; equality should be obtained. Speaking of King Benjamin, a Book of Mormon prophet, Nibley noted:

> He insisted that anyone who withheld his substance from the needy, no matter how improvident and deserving of their fate they might be, "hath great cause to repent," (Mosiah 4:16-18), explaining his position in ringing words: "For behold, are we not all beggars?" (Mosiah 4:19). His son Mosiah wrote equality in the constitution, "that every

man should have an equal chance throughout all the land. . . . " (Mosiah 29:38). "I desire," said the King, "that this inequality should be no more in this land of liberty, and every man may enjoy his rights and privileges alike. . . . " (Mosiah 29:32). This does not mean that some should support others in idleness, "but that the burden should come upon all the people, that every man might bear his part" (Mosiah 29:34) (ibid., 396).

Unlike most other Mormon neo-orthodox theologians, Nibley assumed government—even a strong central government—must accept its role in eliminating poverty and protecting minority interests. There were periods, he observed, when Book of Mormon peoples lamented the loss of a "strong central government in the interests of unlimited ambition" (ibid., 404). For government to levy taxes, especially to eliminate poverty and inequalities, is legitimate. Indeed, this use of taxation, wrote Nibley, is "a means of implementing the principle of equality. Whenever taxation is denounced in the Book of Mormon, it's always because the taxer uses the funds not to help others but for his own aggrandizement" (ibid., 396).

That government may legitimately enact and enforce civil rights legislation to protect "unpopular and weak minorities" is also evident. Sounding as though he were criticizing the social ethics of other Mormon neo-orthodox theologians, Nibley wrote:

> Some have felt that the attempt of the state to implement the ideas of liberty and equality by passing and enforcing laws repugnant to a majority or minority, i.e., laws restraining persecution, discrimination, slavery, and

all violence whatever, is an infringement of free agency. But plainly the Nephites did not think so. As we have seen, they believed that no one was ever without his free agency: one can sin or do unrighteously under any form of government whatever; . . . Since no one can ever make us sin or do right, our free agency is never in the slightest danger. But free institutions and civil liberties are, as history shows, in constant danger. They are even attacked by those who would justify their actions as a defense of free agency, and insist that artificial barriers erected by law to protect the rights of unpopular and weak minorities are an attempt to limit that agency (ibid., 388-89).

Both Mormon-owned Brigham Young University, where Nibley is a professor emeritus, and the Mormon community in general have been the object of Nibley's biting social critique (1978a; 1978b). In a 1983 BYU commencement address, Nibley explained cultural decline, presumably in the church and society, as a consequence of the shift from "leaders to managers." He declared: "Leaders are movers and shakers, original, inventive, unpredictable, imaginative, full of surprises that discomfit the enemy in war and the main office in peace." Managers, however, "are safe, conservative, predictable, conforming organizational men and team players, dedicated to the establishment." While leaders enjoy "a passion for equality," managers find the principle "repugnant" and "counter-productive." The dominance of managers is associated with inordinate materialism in which value is equated with price. Thus, the "manager 'knows the price of everything and the value of nothing,' because for him the value *is* the price" (Nibley

1983, 19). A perverse materialism has become the primary problem confronting the contemporary church and society with this increasing preoccupation with wealth, status, and power.

Given his social critique, Nibley differs from other Mormon neo-orthodox theologians who seem obsessed with anti-Communism, the extension of the franchise, governmental regulation of business, government intervention in civil rights and social relations, and the expansion of the "welfare state." Where other Mormon neo-orthodox theologians see governmental intrusion, Nibley has found political and social responsibility. In this sense, he has more in common with Protestant than Mormon neo-orthodox theologians.

The social climate of contemporary Mormonism, including its rapid growth, enhances prospects for the spread of Mormon neo-orthodoxy. When Catholic sociologist Thomas F. O'Dea justified the study of Mormonism in the late 1950s as a means of better understanding American society, there was little reason to anticipate the phenomenal growth of the church's influence or membership. This remarkable "success" has led some non-Mormon scholars, especially historian Jan Shipps (1985) and sociologist Rodney Stark (1984), to write of Mormonism as a "new world faith." Indeed, it is so significant to Stark that he claimed Mormonism to be "the most important case on the agenda of the social scientific study of religion" (1984, 26).

However, this growth has also presented a problem

for Mormonism. It has raised the ire of Protestant fundamentalists and generated new charges that Mormons are
not Christians. Some scholars feel that the antagonism precludes any serious political cooperation between two groups
sharing "profamily-antifeminist" ideology (see Brinkerhoff,
Jacob, and Mackie 1985; Mauss and Bradford 1985). Though
other scholars doubt that these differences doom potential
coalition (see Shupe and Heinerman 1985; White 1986),
there is clear agreement, supported by survey research, that
young Protestant fundamentalists perceive Mormonism as
an anti-Christian cult (Brinkerhoff et al. 1985). Ironically,
Shipps's sympathetic study of Mormonism may reinforce
this phenomenon. She argues that Mormonism emerged
from Christianity in a fashion analogous to Christianity's
emergence from Judaism. While Mormonism retained much
of its Christian heritage, it became a qualitatively new religion.

The discontent of some former members of the Mormon church, such as Ex-Mormons for Jesus and Jerald and
Sandra Tanner's Utah Lighthouse Ministry, reinforces these
impressions. For example, in *The Changing World of Mormonism*, the Tanners employed my original analysis of traditional Mormonism (1967) to support their argument that
Mormonism is "anti-Christian" (1980, 192-93, 550-52). This
argument obviously rests upon provincial evangelical Protestant assumptions regarding the essence of Christianity.

A quest for respectability, the pursuit of converts,
and expansion of Mormonism throughout the world tempt

contemporary Mormons, especially officials, to present Mormonism as mainline Christianity. Gordon Shepherd and Gary Shepherd (1985a) document a trend toward typical Christian themes in LDS General Conference speeches that is consistent with a renewed emphasis on Christ as the center of Mormonism. Moreover, this tendency is evident in the recent decision by church officials to expand the title of the Book of Mormon to include the subtitle: Another Testament of Jesus Christ. On a more popular level, the jacket of Paul Toscano's 1983 *Gospel Letters to a Mormon Missionary* suggests that the central message that Christ and his atonement are at the heart of the gospel is "a timely proposition in light of the increasing number of claims, made by critics of The Church of Jesus Christ of Latter-day Saints, that Mormons are not Christians." Consequently, the Mormon neo-orthodox emphasis on the cross of Christ rather than the life of Jesus, the depravity of human beings rather than the goodness of humanity, and salvation by grace rather than exaltation by merit may be simply too seductive for those Mormons seeking to "reclaim" their Christian roots.

If Stark's placing of Mormonism at the top of the agenda for the social scientific study of religion grew out of his work on the church's growth, it rests primarily on his concern with the social factors affecting the success or failure of religious movements. I am confident that Mormon success generally, not simply its recruitment processes, derives from its integration of the sacred and secular—in short, from the synthesis of traditional Mormonism that Mormon neo-orthodoxy threatens. Whatever the outcome of the continuing confrontation between these two theologies, I believe few things portend a more ominous future for Mormonism than the loss of that fundamental insight of traditional Mormonism that a religion that cannot save humanity in this life can hardly be expected to do so in the next.

BIBLIOGRAPHY.

The past two decades have witnessed an explosion in Mormon scholarship. Those Mormon neo-orthodox theologians who remain firmly committed to the theology described in this book currently enjoy greater institutional support from the apparent resurgence of anti-intellectualism and authoritarianism among some church officials, who have tended to reinforce neo-orthodox doctrine in both substance and language (see Norman 1985 and Robson 1980, who identify neo-orthodox propensities in the works of McConkie and Maxwell). At the same time, significant scholarship within the church promises to bring issues implicit in the rise of Mormon neo-orthodoxy into the public arena. Indeed, this process has already begun in scholarly Mormon journals, such as *Dialogue: A Journal of Mormon Thought, Sunstone, The Journal of Mormon History, The Journal of the John Whitmer Historical Association,* and, to a lesser extent, *Brigham Young University Studies,* in which a generation of Mormon scholars have explored the strengths and weaknesses of their theology.

I will identify several published essays that are particularly relevant to issues related to the neo-orthodox phenomenon. Articles on the historical development of traditional Mormon theology, such as those by Thomas G.

Alexander (1980) and T. Edgar Lyon (1975), are especially illuminating. The role of Joseph Smith's controversial "King Follett Discourse," in which he publicly proclaimed the necessity of human existence and the eternal progression of God, is discussed at length by Stan Larson (1978), Donald Cannon (1978), and Van Hale (1978). Hale also addressed the reception the sermon has received among RLDS and LDS officials in an article published in 1983. Other historical analyses of the Mormon concept of God include those by Boyd Kirkland (1984; 1986), Van Hale (1985), David John Buerger (1982), and, tangentially, Gary James Bergera (1980).

As previously noted, some scholars have argued that traditional Mormonism, especially its concept of a finite God, is in an enviable position for addressing the problem of evil. While McMurrin, Edwards, and Ostler have made this point and hinted at guidelines, the development of a Mormon theodicy has yet to be accomplished. Still, a careful reading of Peter Appleby's brief but superb essay, "Finitist Theology and the Problem of Evil" (1981), indicates how much even traditional Mormonism may have to abandon to ensure logical consistency.

Increasingly sophisticated analyses of the philosophical and theological difficulties inherent in Mormon theology are supplementing the work of McMurrin, Edwards, and Ostler. The implications of Alfred North Whitehead's philosophy for Mormon metaphysics have been explored by Floyd Ross (1982) and Garland Tickemyer (1984). Mor-

mon philosopher Kent Robson has raised a number of crucial philosophical problems for both traditional and neo-
orthodox Mormonism in such essays as "Time and
Omniscience in Mormon Theology" (1980), "The Foundations of Freedom in Mormon Thought" (1982), and "Omnis
on the Horizon" (1983). While Kim McCall explores ethics
in "What Is Moral Obligation within Mormon Theology?"
(1981), Keith Norman raises important questions regarding a theory of the Atonement, the meaning of the
Godhead, and the relationship of human beings to Jesus in
"Toward a Mormon Christology" (1985).

The foregoing identification is not intended to be
comprehensive. On the contrary, it merely functions to indicate issues and problems of growing interest to Mormon
scholars. Working within the tradition itself, these intellectuals are addressing philosophical and theological problems
of particular relevance to ecclesiastical officials and Mormon neo-orthodox theologians. Though they lack institutional support and sometimes encounter censure, their commitment to both the Mormon tradition and responsible
scholarship is nonetheless reinforced by the growing popularity of such forums as the annual Sunstone Theological
Symposium held in Salt Lake City, Washington, D.C., and
California.

While the scholars dealing with these philosophical
and theological issues are almost exclusively Mormon, the
preoccupation with anthropological, historical, political, and
sociological questions has spread to non-Mormon scholars.

Articles by Mormons and non-Mormons frequently appear in social science journals, for example, and books by both are published with increasing regularity by academic and commercial presses (see Mauss 1984; Mauss and Franks 1984). This improvement in the quality of scholarship and burgeoning interest in the Mormon phenomenon promise to render the coming decades the most intellectually stimulating in Mormon history.

ADORNO, T. W., et al. *The Authoritarian Personality.* New York: Harper and Row, 1950.

ALEXANDER, THOMAS G. "The Reconstruction of Mormon Doctrine: From Joseph Smith to Progressive Theology." *Sunstone* 5 (July-Aug. 1980): 24–33.

ALLEN, MARK K. "Personality and Cultural Factors Related to Religious Authoritarianism." Ph.D. diss., Stanford University, 1955.

ALLRED, JANICE M. "Toward a Mormon Concept of Original Sin." *Sunstone* 8 (May-June 1983): 13–18.

ANDERSON, NELS. *Desert Saints.* Chicago: University of Chicago Press, 1966.

ANDRUS, HYRUM. "The Greatness and Majesty of God." *The Doctrine and Covenants and Man's Relationship to Deity.* Provo, UT: Brigham Young University Extension Division, 1960.

——————. "Joseph Smith's Idea of the Gospel." *Seminar on the Prophet Joseph Smith.* Provo, UT: Brigham Young University Adult Education and Extension Services, 1961.

——————. *Liberalism, Conservatism, and Mormonism.* Salt Lake City: Deseret, 1965.

——————. *Doctrinal Commentary on the Pearl of Great Price.* Salt Lake City: Deseret Book, 1967.

APPLEBY, PETER. "Finitist Theology and the Problem of Evil."
    Sunstone 6 (Nov.-Dec. 1981): 52–54.

ARONSON, ELLIOT. *The Social Animal*. San Francisco: Freeman, 1972.

ARRINGTON, LEONARD J. *Great Basin Kingdom*. Lincoln: University of Nebraska Press, 1966.

————. "The Intellectual Tradition of the Latter-day Saints."
    Dialogue: A Journal of Mormon Thought 4 (Spring 1969).

BARON, SALO W., AND JOSEPH L. BLAU. *Judaism: Postbiblical
    and Talmudic Period*. Indianapolis: The Liberal Arts Press, 1954.

BARTH, KARL. *The Word of God and the Word of Man*. Translated by
    Douglas Horton. New York: Harper and Row, 1957.

————. *Dogmatics in Outline*. New York: Harper and Row, 1959.

————. *The Humanity of God*. Richmond: John Knox Press, 1960.

————. *Christ and Adam*. Translated by T. A. Smail. New York:
    Crowell-Collier Publishing, 1962.

BELL, DANIEL. "The Dispossessed." *The Radical Right*. Edited by
    Daniel Bell. New York: Doubleday and Co., 1963.

BENNION, LOWELL L. "The Nature of Man in Mormon Theology."
    An interfaith discussion on the nature of man, 2 Dec. 1965,
    Salt Lake City.

BENSON, EZRA TAFT. *The Internal Threat to the American Way of
    Life*. Salt Lake City: Bookcraft, 1961.

————. "Vietnam—Victory or Surrender." *Speeches of the
    Year*. Provo, UT: Brigham Young University, 1969.

————. "Fourteen Fundamentals in Following the Prophets."
    A speech to the Brigham Young University Devotional Assembly, 26 Feb. 1980, Provo, UT.

BERGER, PETER. *The Sacred Canopy*. Garden City, NY: Doubleday,
    1967.

BERGERA, GARY JAMES. "The Orson Pratt/Brigham Young Controversies: Conflict Within the Quorums, 1853–1868." *Dialogue: A Journal of Mormon Thought* 13 (Summer 1980): 7–49.

—————. "Grey Matters." *Dialogue: A Journal of Mormon Thought* 15 (Spring 1982): 178–83.

—————, AND RONALD L. PRIDDIS. *Brigham Young University: A House of Faith.* Salt Lake City: Signature Books, 1985.

BOOK OF MORMON. Salt Lake City: Church of Jesus Christ of Latter-day Saints, 1966.

BOYD, GEORGE T. "The Moral Nature of Man." A paper presented to the LDS Institute and Seminary Convention, 1962, Brigham Young University, Provo, UT.

BRINKERHOFF, MERLIN B. JEFFERY C. JACOB, AND MARLENE M. MACKIE. "Mormonism and the Moral Majority Make Strange Bedfellows: An Exploratory Critique." Paper presented to the Pacific Sociological Association, Albuquerque, NM, 1985.

BRODIE, FAWN M. *No Man Knows My History.* New York: Alfred A. Knopf, 1945.

BROWN, ROBERT McAFEE. "A New Step in Understanding." *Dialogue: A Journal of Mormon Thought* 1 (Spring 1966).

BRUNNER, H. EMIL. *The Theology of Crisis.* New York: Charles Scribner's Sons, 1929.

—————. *Our Faith.* Translated by John Rilling. New York: Charles Scribner's Sons, 1936.

—————. *Man in Revolt.* Translated by Olive Wyon. London: Lutterworth Press, 1939.

BUERGER, DAVID JOHN. "The Adam-God Doctrine." *Dialogue: A Journal of Mormon Thought* 15 (Spring 1982): 14–58.

BUSH, LESTER. "Mormonism's Negro Doctrine: An Historical Overview." *Dialogue: A Journal of Mormon Thought* 8 (Spring 1973): 11–68.

—————. "Birth Control Among the Mormons: Introduction to

an Insistent Question." *Dialogue: A Journal of Mormon Thought* 10 (Autumn 1976): 12–44.

——————, AND ARMAND L. MAUSS, eds. *Neither White Nor Black*. Salt Lake City: Signature Books, 1984.

BUSHMAN, RICHARD L. *Joseph Smith and the Beginnings of Mormonism*. Urbana: University of Illinois Press, 1984.

CALVIN, JOHN. *On God and Man: Selections from Institutes of the Christian Religion*. Edited by F. W. Strothmann. New York: Frederick Ungar Publishing Co., 1956.

CANNON, DONALD Q. "The King Follett Discourse: Joseph Smith's Greatest Sermon in Historical Perspective." *Brigham Young University Studies* 18 (Winter 1978): 179–92.

CANTRIL, HADLEY. *The Psychology of Social Movements*. New York: John Wiley and Sons, 1963.

CASALIS, GEORGES. *Portrait of Karl Barth*. Translated by Robert McAfee Brown. New York: Doubleday, 1963.

CHRISTENSEN, HAROLD T. "The Persistence of Chastity: A Built-in Resistance within Mormon Culture to Secular Trends." *Sunstone* 7 (March-April 1982): 7–14.

——————, AND KENNETH L. CANNON. "The Fundamentalist Emphasis at Brigham Young University: 1935–1978." *Journal for the Scientific Study of Religion* 17 (March 1978): 53–57.

CLARK, J. REUBEN, JR. "The Chartered Course of the Church in Education." *The Improvement Era* 31 (Sept. 1938).

——————. "The Genius of Our Church Organization." An address to Seminary and Institute Faculty, Brigham Young University, Provo, UT, 17 June 1958.

CLOWARD, RICHARD A. "Illegitimate Means, Anomie, and Deviant Behavior." *American Sociological Review* 24 (April 1959).

CR. *Conference Report of the Church of Jesus Christ of Latter-day*

Saints. Salt Lake City: Church of Jesus Christ of Latter-day
     Saints, published semiannually in April and October.

CROSS, WHITNEY R. *The Burned-Over District.* Ithaca: Cornell Uni-
     versity Press, 1950.

D&C. Doctrine and Covenants of the Church of Jesus Christ of Latter-
     day Saints. Salt Lake City: Church of Jesus Christ of Latter-
     day Saints, 1958. Followed by section and verse numbers.

DILLENBERGER, JOHN, AND CLAUDE WELCH. *Protestant Chris-
     tianity.* New York: Charles Scribner's Sons, 1954.

DURKHEIM, EMILE. *Suicide.* Edited by George Simpson. Glencoe:
     Free Press, 1951.

EDWARDS, PAUL M. "Persistences that Differ: Comments on the
     Doctrine of Man." *Sunstone* 5 (Sept.-Oct. 1980): 44–49.

———. *Preface to Faith: A Philosophical Inquiry into RLDS
     Beliefs.* Salt Lake City: Signature Books, 1984.

ERICKSEN, EPHRAIM E. *The Psychological and Ethical Aspect of Mor-
     mon Group Life.* Chicago: University of Chicago Press, 1922.
     Reprt. 1975. Salt Lake City: University of Utah Press.

FESTINGER, LEON. *A Theory of Cognitive Dissonance.* Stanford:
     Stanford University Press, 1957.

———, et al. *When Prophecy Fails.* New York: Harper and Row,
     1965.

FREUD, SIGMUND. *Civilization and It Discontents.* New York: Norton,
     1961.

———. *The Future of an Illusion.* Garden City, NY: Anchor,
     1964.

———. *Moses and Monotheism.* New York: Vintage, 1939.

———. *Totem and Taboo.* New York: Vintage, 1918.

FROMM, ERICH. *Escape From Freedom.* New York: Rinehart, 1941.

GENTRY, LELAND H. "What of the Lectures on Faith?" *Brigham
     Young University Studies* 19 (Fall 1978): 5–19.

GOTTLIEB, ROBERT, AND PETER WILEY. *America's Saints: The Rise of Mormon Power.* New York: G. P. Putnam's Sons, 1984.

HADDEN, JEFFERY K. "Toward Desacralizing Secularization Theory." *Social Forces* 65 (March 1987): 587–611.

HALE, VAN. "The Doctrinal Impact of the King Follett Discourse." *Brigham Young University Studies* 18 (Winter 1978): 209–25.

——————. "The King Follett Discourse: Textual History and Criticism." *Sunstone* 8 (Sept.-Oct. 1983): 4–12.

——————. "Defining the Mormon Doctrine of Deity." *Sunstone* 10 (Jan. 1985): 23–27.

HANSEN, KLAUS. *Quest for Empire.* Lincoln: University of Nebraska Press, 1974.

HARDY, KENNETH. "Social Origins of American Scientists and Scholars." *Science* 185 (1974): 497–506.

HARRIS, MARVIN. *Cows, Pigs, Wars, and Witches.* New York: Random House, 1974.

HEATON, TIM B., AND SANDRA CALKINS. "Contraceptive Use Among Mormons, 1965–75." *Dialogue: A Journal of Mormon Thought* 16 (Autumn 1983): 106–109.

HEINERMAN, JOHN, AND ANSON SHUPE. *The Mormon Corporate Empire.* Boston: Beacon Press, 1985.

HOFSTADTER, RICHARD. "The Pseudo-Conservative Revolt (1955)." *The Radical Right.* Edited by Daniel Bell. New York: Doubleday and Co., 1963.

IGNATIUS. "To the Romans." *The Apostolic Fathers.* Translated by Francis Climm, Joseph Marigue, and Gerald Walsh. New York: Cima Publishing Co., 1947.

JD. *Journal of Discourses.* 26 vols. Liverpool: Latter-day Saints' Book Depot, 1854–86. Followed by volume and page numbers.

KENNEY, SCOTT G. "Personal and Social Morality in a Religious

Context: Reinhold Niebuhr and the Mormon Experience."
Sunstone 5 (March-April 1980): 19–23.

KIRKLAND, BOYD. "Jehovah as the Father: The Development of the
Mormon Jehovah Doctrine." *Sunstone* 9 (Autumn 1984): 36–44.

──────── . "Elohim and Jehovah in Mormonism and the Bible."
Dialogue: A Journal of Mormon Thought 19 (Spring 1986): 77–93.

LARSON, STAN. "The King Follett Sermon: A Newly Amalgamated
Text." *Brigham Young University Studies* 18 (Winter 1978):
193–208.

LEONE, MARK. *The Roots of Modern Mormonism.* Cambridge: Harvard
University Press, 1984.

LUDLOW, DANIEL. "Our Divine Destiny—A Third Dimensional
View." *Speeches of the Year.* Provo, UT: Brigham Young University Press, 1970.

LYON, T. EDGAR. "Doctrinal Development of the Church During
the Nauvoo Sojourn, 1839–1846." *Brigham Young University
Studies* 15 (Summer 1975): 435–46.

MACKINTOSH, H. R. *Types of Modern Theology.* New York: Charles
Scribner's Sons, 1937.

MACQUARRIE, JOHN. *Twentieth Century Religious Thought.* New
York: Harper and Row, 1963.

MANNHEIM, KARL. *Ideology and Utopia.* Translated by Louis Writh
and Edward Shills. New York: Harcourt, Brace and World,
1936.

MARX, KARL. *Capital.* Translated by E. Unterman. Chicago: C. H.
Kerr, 1909.

──────── . *The Poverty of Philosophy.* New York: International Pub-
lishers, 1963.

──────── . *Selected Writings in Sociology and Social Philosophy.* Translated by T. B. Bottomore and edited by T. B. Bottomore and
M. Rubel. New York: McGraw-Hill, 1964.

MAUSS, ARMAND L. "Shall the Youth of Zion Falter? Mormon Youth and Sex: A Two-City Comparison." *Dialogue: A Journal of Mormon Thought* 10 (Autumn 1976): 82–84.

——————. "The Fading of the Pharoah's Curse: The Decline and Fall of the Priesthood Ban against Blacks in the Mormon Church." *Dialogue: A Journal of Mormon Thought* 14 (Autumn 1981): 10–45.

——————. "White on Black among the Mormons: A Critique of White and White." *Sociological Analysis* 42 (Fall 1982): 277–82.

——————. "Sociological Perspectives on the Mormon Subculture." *Annual Review of Sociology* 10 (1984): 437–60.

——————, and Jeffrey R. Franks. "Comprehensive Bibliography of Social Science Literature on the Mormons." *Review of Religious Research* 26 (Sept. 1984): 73–115.

——————, and M. Gerald Bradford. "Mormon Assimilation and Politics: Toward a Theory of Mormon Church Involvement in National U.S. Politics." Paper presented to Society for the Scientific Study of Religion, Savannah, GA, 1985.

MAXWELL, NEAL A. "A More Determined Discipleship." *Ensign* 9 (Feb. 1979a): 69–73.

——————. *All These Things Shall Give Thee Experience.* Salt Lake City: Deseret Book, 1979b.

McCALL, KIM. "What Is Moral Obligation within Mormon Theology?" *Sunstone* 6 (Nov.-Dec. 1981): 27–31.

McCONKIE, BRUCE R. *Mormon Doctrine.* Salt Lake City: Bookcraft, 1958. 2nd. Edition 1966.

——————. "All Are Alike Unto God." An address to LDS Seminary and Institute Faculty, 18 Aug. 1978, Brigham Young University, Provo, UT.

——————. "The Lord God of the Restoration." *Ensign* 10 (Nov. 1980).

————. "The Seven Deadly Heresies." *Brigham Young University 1981–82 Fireside and Devotional Speeches.* Provo, UT: Brigham Young University, 1982.

MCKAY, DAVID O. *Statements on Communism and the United States.* Salt Lake City: Deseret Book, 1964.

McKINLAY, LYNN. "For Behold Ye Are Free." *Know Your Religion Series.* Provo, UT: Brigham Young University, n.d.

McMURRIN, STERLING M. *The Theological Foundations of the Mormon Religion.* Salt Lake City: University of Utah Press, 1965.

MERTON, ROBERT K. "Social Structure and Anomie." *Social Theory and Social Structure.* Glencoe: Free Press, 1957.

NELSON, LOWRY. *In the Direction of His Dreams.* New York: Philosophical Library, 1985.

NELSON, RUSSELL M. "Truth and More." An address to faculty at Brigham Young University, 27 Aug. 1985, Provo, UT.

NIBLEY, HUGH. *The World and the Prophets.* Salt Lake City: Deseret, 1954.

————. "Nobody to Blame." An open letter to "Brother Bergin," 29 July 1960.

————. *Since Cumorah.* Salt Lake City: Deseret Book, 1969.

————. "The Best Possible Test." *Dialogue: A Journal of Mormon Thought* 8 (Spring 1973): 73–77.

————. "Educating the Saints." *Nibley On the Timely and the Timeless.* Provo, UT: Religious Studies Center, Brigham Young University, 1978a.

————. "Zeal Without Knowledge." *Nibley on the Timely and the Timeless.* Provo, UT: Religious Studies Center, Brigham Young University, 1978b.

————. "Leaders to Managers: The Fatal Shift." *Dialogue: A Journal of Mormon Thought* 16 (Winter 1983): 12–21.

NIEBUHR, REINHOLD. *Moral Man and Immoral Society.* New York: Charles Scribner's Sons, 1932.

——————. *Reflections of the End of an Era.* New York: Charles Scriber's Sons, 1934.

——————. *The Children of Light and the Children of Darkness.* New York: Charles Scribner's Sons, 1944.

——————. "The Religious Situation in America." *Religion and Contemporary Society.* Edited by Harold Stahmer. New York: Macmillan, 1963.

NIEBUHR, H. RICHARD. *The Social Sources of Denominationalism.* Cleveland: The World Publishing Company, 1929.

"A 1945 Perspective." *Dialogue: A Journal of Mormon Thought* 19 (Spring 1986): 35–39.

NORMAN, KEITH E. "Toward a Mormon Christology." *Sunstone* 10 (April 1985): 19–25.

OAKS, DALLIN H. "Reading Church History." An address delivered at the 1985 CES Doctrine and Covenants Symposium, 16 Aug. 1985, Brigham Young University, Provo, UT.

O'DEA, THOMAS F. *The Mormons.* Chicago: University of Chicago Press, 1957.

——————. *The Sociology of Religion.* Englewood Cliffs, NJ: Prentice-Hall, 1966.

——————. "The Crisis in American Religious Consciousness." *Daedalus,* Winter 1967.

——————. "Sources of Strain in Mormon History Reconsidered." *Mormonism and American Culture.* Edited by Marvin Hill and James B. Allen. New York: Harper and Row, 1972.

——————, and Renato Poblete. *American Catholic Sociological Review* 21 (Spring 1960): 18–36.

OLSON, DONALD P. "Understanding the Scope of the Grace of Christ." *Sunstone* 9 (Autumn 1984): 21–25.

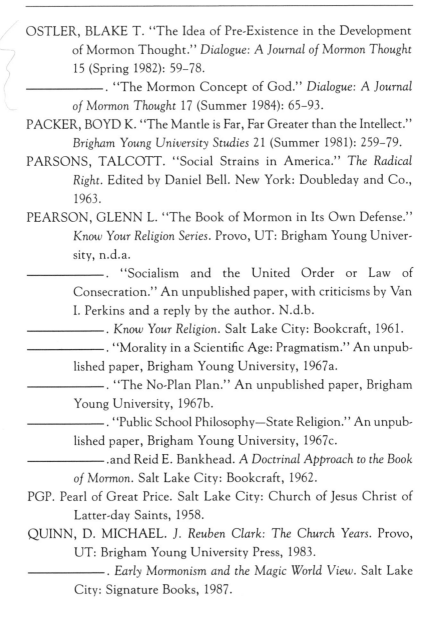

OSTLER, BLAKE T. "The Idea of Pre-Existence in the Development of Mormon Thought." *Dialogue: A Journal of Mormon Thought* 15 (Spring 1982): 59–78.

————. "The Mormon Concept of God." *Dialogue: A Journal of Mormon Thought* 17 (Summer 1984): 65–93.

PACKER, BOYD K. "The Mantle is Far, Far Greater than the Intellect." *Brigham Young University Studies* 21 (Summer 1981): 259–79.

PARSONS, TALCOTT. "Social Strains in America." *The Radical Right*. Edited by Daniel Bell. New York: Doubleday and Co., 1963.

PEARSON, GLENN L. "The Book of Mormon in Its Own Defense." *Know Your Religion Series*. Provo, UT: Brigham Young University, n.d.a.

————. "Socialism and the United Order or Law of Consecration." An unpublished paper, with criticisms by Van I. Perkins and a reply by the author. N.d.b.

————. *Know Your Religion*. Salt Lake City: Bookcraft, 1961.

————. "Morality in a Scientific Age: Pragmatism." An unpublished paper, Brigham Young University, 1967a.

————. "The No-Plan Plan." An unpublished paper, Brigham Young University, 1967b.

————. "Public School Philosophy—State Religion." An unpublished paper, Brigham Young University, 1967c.

————.and Reid E. Bankhead. *A Doctrinal Approach to the Book of Mormon*. Salt Lake City: Bookcraft, 1962.

PGP. Pearl of Great Price. Salt Lake City: Church of Jesus Christ of Latter-day Saints, 1958.

QUINN, D. MICHAEL. *J. Reuben Clark: The Church Years*. Provo, UT: Brigham Young University Press, 1983.

————. *Early Mormonism and the Magic World View*. Salt Lake City: Signature Books, 1987.

RECTOR, HARTMAN, JR. "Let Us Stand Up for Freedom." *Speeches of the Year*. Provo, UT: Brigham Young University Press, 1969.

REISMAN, DAVID. "Intellectuals and Discontented Classes (1962)." *The Radical Right*. Edited by Daniel Bell. New York: Doubleday and Co., 1963.

RIDDLE, CHAUNCEY. "The Conservative View in Mormonism." A discussion with Lowell L. Bennion at Brigham Young University, Provo, UT. N.d.

——————. "Freedom." An address to Young Americans for Freedom, Brigham Young University, Provo, UT, 1965.

——————. "Letter to Michael." *Ensign* 5 (Sept. 1975): 79–84.

ROBERTS, B. H. *The Gospel and Man's Relationship to Deity*. Rev. ed. Salt Lake City: George Q. Cannon & Sons, 1893.

——————. "The 'Mormon' Doctrine of Deity." *Improvement Era* 6 (Jan. 1903).

——————. *A Comprehensive History of the Church of Jesus Christ of Latter-day Saints, Century I*. 6 vols. Salt Lake City: Deseret News Press, 1930.

ROBSON, KENT. "Time and Omniscience in Mormon Theology." *Sunstone* 5 (May-June 1980): 17–23.

——————. "The Foundations of Freedom in Mormon Thought." *Sunstone* 7 (Sept.-Oct. 1982): 51–54.

——————. "Omnis on the Horizon." *Sunstone* 8 (July-Aug. 1983): 21–23.

ROKEACH, MILTON. *The Open and Closed Mind*. New York: Basic Books, 1960.

ROSS, FLOYD M. "Process Philosophy and Mormon Thought." *Sunstone* 7 (Jan.-Feb. 1982): 16–27.

RYRIE, CHARLES C. *Neo-Orthodoxy*. Chicago: Moody Bible Institute, 1966.

RYTTING, MARVIN, AND ANN RYTTING. "Exhortations for Chastity: A Content Analysis of Church Literature." *Sunstone* 7 (March-April 1982): 15-21.

SHEPHERD, GORDON, AND GARY SHEPHERD. *A Kingdom Transformed: Themes in the Development of Mormonism.* Salt Lake City: University of Utah Press, 1984a.

——————. "Mormonism in Secular Society: Changing Patterns in Official Ecclesiastical Rhetoric." *Review of Religious Research* 26 (Sept. 1984b).

SHIPPS, JAN. *Mormonism: The Story of a New Religious Tradition.* Urbana: University of Illinois Press, 1985.

SHUPE, ANSON, AND JOHN HEINERMAN. "Mormonism and the New Christian Right: An Emergent Coalition?" *Review of Religious Research* 27 (Dec. 1985): 146-57.

SMITH, JOSEPH. *Lectures on Faith.* Compiled by Nels B. Lundwall. Salt Lake City: Nels B. Lundwall, n.d.

——————. "King Follett Discourse." *Teachings of the Prophet Joseph Smith.* Compiled by Joseph Fielding Smith. Salt Lake City: Deseret News Press, 1938.

SMITH, JOSEPH FIELDING. *Doctrines of Salvation.* Vol. 1. Compiled by Bruce R. McConkie. Salt Lake City: Bookcraft, 1954.

——————. *Answers to Gospel Questions.* Vol. 2. Salt Lake City: Deseret Book, 1958.

SMITH, WILFORD E. "Mormon Sexual Standards on College Campuses: Or Deal Us Out of the Sexual Revolution." *Dialogue: A Journal of Mormon Thought* 10 (Autumn 1976): 76-81.

STARK, RODNEY. "The Rise of a New World Faith." *Review of Religious Research* 26 (Sept. 1984): 18-27.

SWANSON, GUY E. "Modern Secularity: Its Meaning, Sources, and Interpretation." *The Religious Situation: 1968.* Edited by Donald Cutler. Boston: Beacon Press, 1968.

TALMAGE, JAMES E. *A Study of the Articles of Faith*. 33rd ed. Salt Lake City: Church of Jesus Christ of Latter-day Saints, 1955.

TANNER, JERALD, AND SANDRA TANNER. *The Changing World of Mormonism*. Chicago: Moody Press, 1980.

THORNDIKE, E. L. "The Origins of Superior Men." *Scientific Monthly* 56 (May 1943): 424–32.

TICKEMYER, GARLAND E. "Joseph Smith and Process Theology." *Dialogue: A Journal of Mormon Thought* 17 (Autumn 1984): 75–85.

TILLICH, PAUL. *The Religious Situation*. Translated by Richard Niebuhr. New York: Meridian Books, 1932.

——————. *Biblical Religion and the Search for Ultimate Reality*. Chicago: University of Chicago Press, 1955.

TOSCANO, MARGARET MERRILL. "Beyond Matriarchy, Beyond Patriarchy: Christ as Mediator of the Marriage Covenant." Paper presented at the Eighth Annual Sunstone Theological Symposium, Salt Lake City, UT, 21 Aug. 1986.

TOSCANO, PAUL J. *Letters to a Mormon Missionary*. Provo, UT: Grandin Book, 1983.

——————. "Divine Marriage." Paper presented at the Eighth Annual Sunstone Theological Symposium, Salt Lake City, UT, 21 Aug. 1986.

TURNER, RODNEY. "The Position of Adam in Latter-day Saint Scripture and Theology." M.A. thesis, Brigham Young University, 1953.

TURNER, WALLACE. *The Mormon Establishment*. Cambridge: Houghton Mifflin, 1966.

VOROS, J. FREDERIC, JR. "What is Man?" Paper delivered to Ricks College Honors Program, 15 Nov. 1978.

——————. "Was the Book of Mormon Buried with King Follett?"

Paper presented at the Seventh Annual Sunstone Theological Symposium, Salt Lake City, UT, 23 Aug. 1985.

WEBER, MAX. *The Protestant Ethic and the Spirit of Capitalism*. Translated by Talcott Parsons. New York: Charles Scribner's Sons, 1958.

————. *The Sociology of Religion*. Translated by Ephraim Fischoff. Boston: Beacon Press, 1963.

WESTHUES, KENNETH. "Secularization Theory and Organizations Theory: A Synthesis and a Test." Ph.D. diss., Vanderbilt University, 1969.

WHITE, O. KENDALL, JR. "The Social Psychological Basis of Mormon New-Orthodoxy." M.S. thesis, University of Utah, 1967.

————. "Mormonism-A Nineteenth Century Heresy." *The Journal of Religious Thought* 26 (Spring-Summer 1969): 44–55.

————. "The Transformation of Mormon Theology." *Dialogue: A Journal of Mormon Thought* 5 (Summer 1970):9–24.

————. "A Reply to Critics of the Mormon Neo-Orthodoxy Hypothesis." *Dialogue: A Journal of Mormon Thought* 6 (Fall 1971a): 97–100.

————. "Mormon Neo-Orthodox Theology." *The Journal of Religious Thought* 28 (Autumn-Winter 1971b): 119–31.

————. "Mormonism's Anti-Black Policy and Prospects for Change." *The Journal of Religious Thought* 29 (Autumn-Winter 1972): 39–60.

————. "Mormonism in America and Canada: Accommodation to the Nation-State." *The Canadian Journal of Sociology*, 4 (Spring 1978): 161–81.

————. "Mormon Resistance and Accomodation: From Communitarian Socialism to Corporate Capitalism." *Self-Help in Urban America: Patterns of Minority Economic Development*. Edited by Scott Cummings. Port Washington: Kennikat Press, 1980.

————. "Overt and Covert Politics: The Mormon Church's

Anti-ERA Campaign in Virginia." *Virginia Social Science Journal* 19 (Winter 1984): 11–16.

——————. "A Feminist Challenge: 'Mormons for ERA' as an Internal Social Movement." *The Journal of Ethnic Studies* 13 (Spring 1985): 29–50.

——————. "Ideology of the Family in Nineteenth Century Mormonism." *Sociological Spectrum* 6 (June 1986a): 289–306.

——————. "A Review and Commentary on the Prospects of a Mormon New Christian Right Coalition." *Review of Religious Research* 28 (Dec. 1986b): 180–88.

——————, AND DARYL WHITE. "Abandoning an Unpopular Policy: An Analysis of the Decision Granting the Mormon Priesthood to Blacks." *Sociological Analysis* 41 (Fall 1980): 231–45.

——————. "A Critique of Leone's and Dolgin's Application of Bellah's Evolutionary Model to Mormonism." *Review of Religious Research* 23 (Sept. 1981): 30–44.

——————. "Perpetuating Patriarchy: The Mormon Church's Anti-ERA Campaign." A Paper presented to the Southern Sociological Society, Memphis, TN, 15–17 April 1982a.

——————. "A Reply to Mauss's Critique of Our Analysis of Admitting Blacks into the Mormon Priesthood." *Sociological Analysis* 42 (Fall 1982b): 283–88.

WHITNEY, ORSON F. *Elias—An Epic of the Ages.* Rev. ed. Salt Lake City: Orson F. Whitney, 1914.

WIDTSOE, JOHN A. *A Rational Theology.* 6th ed. Salt Lake City: Deseret Book, 1952.

——————. *Evidences and Reconciliations.* Arranged by G. Homer Durham. Salt Lake City: Bookcraft, 1960.

WILKINSON, ERNEST L. "The Spiritual and Intellectual Training of BYU Students and Their Acceptance in the Market Place." Part of the Commencement Report to the Graduating Class, 27 May 1966, Brigham Young University, Provo, UT.

—————. "Welcome Address." *Speeches of the Year*. Provo, UT: Brigham Young University Press, 1967.

—————. "The Unique Role of BYU Among the Universities of America." *Speeches of the Year*. Provo, UT: Brigham Young University Press, 1970.

YARN, DAVID H. *The Gospel: God, Man, and Truth*. Salt Lake City: Deseret Book, 1965.

YOUNG, BRIGHAM. "Man's Agency." *The Contributor* 11 (Nov. 1889).